P · O · C · K · E · T · S

AIRCRAFT

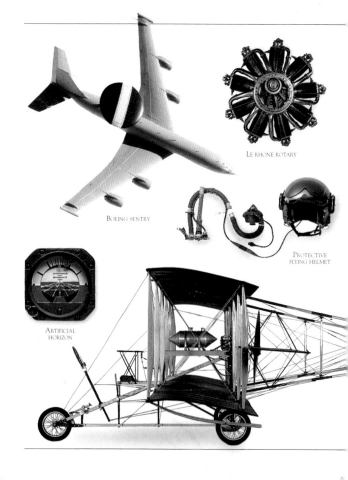

LE RHONE ROTARY

BOEING SENTRY

PROTECTIVE
FLYING HELMET

ARTIFICIAL
HORIZON

P · O · C · K · E · T · S

AIRCRAFT

Written by
DAVID JEFFERIS

C-47 DAKOTA

PEGASUS
ULTRALIGHT

CURTISS MODEL-D
PUSHER

A DK PUBLISHING BOOK

Project editors Anna McMurray
Tim Hetherington
Art editor Martin Wilson
Senior editor Alastair Dougall
Senior art editor Sarah Crouch
Production Josie Alabaster
Picture research Tom Worsley
US editor Constance M. Robinson
US consultant James Ott

First American edition, 1997
2 4 6 8 10 9 7 5 3 1
Published in the United States by
DK Publishing, Inc., 95 Madison Avenue
New York, New York 10016

Visit us on the World Wide Web at http://www.dk.com

Copyright © 1997
Dorling Kindersley Ltd., London

Published in Great Britain by Dorling Kindersley Ltd.

A catalog record is available from the Library of Congress.
ISBN 0-7894-1496-1

Color reproduction by Colorscan, Singapore
Printed and bound in Italy by L.E.G.O.

CONTENTS

HOW TO USE THIS BOOK

These pages show you how to use *Pockets: Aircraft*.
The book is divided into eight sections containing
information on different types of aircraft. There is
also an introductory section at the front, and a
reference section at the back.

ALL ABOUT AIRCRAFT
The aircraft in this book have
been grouped into eight
sections. An introductory page
at the beginning of each section
gives an overview of the pages
that follow. Turn to the contents
pages, index, or glossary for more
information about different
types of aircraft and the history
and future of aviation.

Corner coding

Heading

Introduction

Annotation

Running head

OBSERVATION AND CONTRO
THE FIRST MILITARY AIRCRAFT were World War I
spotter planes. Today, early warning of enemy ai
is as important, but radar and electronic
equipment have replaced simple
observation. The crews of
command aircraft not
only track enemy
movements but also
control and direct
aircraft in response

Part ash
The Grumman E8 of World
have to win may far th
market the observati
enemy activity wa
first radars and mi
build a mazes. The
had two min
is a datan
scree

Fact box

CORNER CODING
The corners of the
main section pages
are color coded to
remind you which
section you are in.

▉ INSIDE AN AIRCRAFT
▉ AIRLINERS
▉ GENERAL AVIATION
▉ COMBAT AIRCRAFT
▉ WAR IN THE AIR
▉ VERTICAL TAKEOFF
▉ NAVIGATION AND SAFETY
▉ THE LEADING EDGE

HEADING
This describes the
subject of the page.
This page is about
radar technology and
enemy surveillance
equipment.

INTRODUCTION
This provides you with a
summary and overview of
the subject. After reading
the introduction, you
should have a clear idea of
what the following page,
or pages, are about.

LABELS
For extra clarity, some
pictures have labels. These
identify a picture
if this is not immediately
obvious from the text.

RUNNING HEADS

These remind you which section you are in. The top of the left-hand page gives the section name, and the top of the right-hand page gives the subject heading. This page on Observation and Control is from the Combat Aircraft section.

FACT BOXES

Many pages have fact boxes. These provide at-a-glance information about a subject, such as when the first observer in a balloon was sent up in the air as a spy, or when the first spotter planes were used against enemy forces.

Label

Caption

REFERENCE SECTION

The reference pages are yellow and appear at the back of the book. On these, you will find a timeline of aircraft and other facts about important people and places in the story of flight. There is a list of aviation museums and air displays on the resources pages.

CAPTIONS AND ANNOTATIONS

Each illustration is accompanied by a caption. Annotations, in *italics*, give more information on the features of an illustration, and there are usually leader lines to point out details of the picture.

INDEX AND GLOSSARY

At the back of the book is an index listing every subject in the book. By referring to the index, information on particular topics can be found quickly. A glossary defines technical terms used in the book.

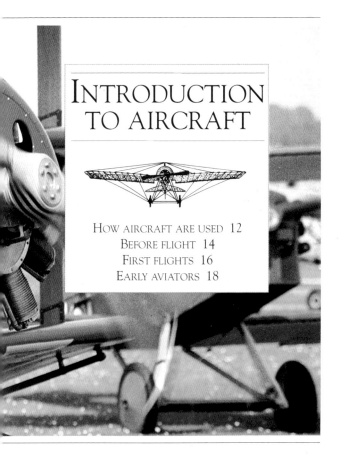

INTRODUCTION TO AIRCRAFT

HOW AIRCRAFT ARE USED

WHEN THE FIRST AVIATORS took to the air earlier this century, they could not have imagined how aircraft would transform the world. Today, a single airport – Chicago's O'Hare – moves 65 million passengers a year. In the military field, aircraft range from fighters and bombers to giant airlifters that can transport entire fighting forces.

The CL-415 is an amphibious aircraft

AIR RESCUE
Helicopters are used for emergency rescues at sea or from cliff tops. A Sea King can fly at a speed of 143 mph (230 km/h) and haul people to safety.

WATER BOMBER
In fire-risk areas, such as scrub land or forest, specialized aircraft are used to tackle the flames. This Canadair CL-415 scoops water from lakes or open water, and drops it as a liquid "bomb" to smother fires.

AIRCRAFT FACTS
• The most successful transport aircraft is the Douglas DC3; 10,926 were built.
• The Concorde cruises at a speed of 1,320 mph (2,125 km/h).

DASSAULT
MIRAGE 2000

Triangular
"delta" wing

Probe for
in-flight
refueling

5-OB

ATTACK MACHINE
All air forces maintain squadrons of attack aircraft.
Here, a French Mirage 2000 jet is ready for action, with
a missile load and long-range fuel tank. To extend its
range, the Mirage uses a refueling probe to take on fuel
from a flying tanker. The Mirage has been one of
France's most successful military aircraft.

Hang gliders
can fly at
speeds as low
as 11 mph
(18 km/h)

BUSINESS JET
The Challenger 604 is one of the largest
"biz-jets" available. Almost all aircraft in
this category have two rear-mounted engines
and swept-wings, and cruise at 500–600 mph
(805–966 km/h). Cockpits and controls are
designed to meet airline standards, and cabin
interiors vary – from standard to superluxury.

GLIDER
Hang gliding is
one of the least
expensive types of
flight. Among the
designs to choose from are
the swept wing and delta
shapes. All gliders have the
same basics: a soft wing
made from nylon fabric and
a lightweight framework.

BEFORE FLIGHT

BEFORE THE 19TH CENTURY, the way to fly seemed to be to copy the flapping motion of a bird's wing. The devices that followed were either too complex to build, too heavy to take off, or both. The answer was pioneered by Englishman Sir George Cayley, whose ideas for a kitelike glider of 1804 have been followed by aircraft designers ever since.

ICARUS
In Greek mythology, Icarus was killed when he flew too close to the Sun. His wings of wax and feathers made by his father, Daedalus, melted.

LEONARDO DA VINCI'S FLYING MACHINE

IN A FLAP
In 1678, a French locksmith named Besnier tried to fly using flaplike wings (although probably larger than the ones shown). Besnier's courageous flight was no more than a barely controlled plummet.

BESNIER

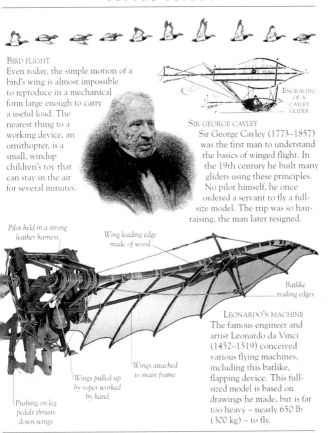

BIRD FLIGHT

Even today, the simple motion of a bird's wing is almost impossible to reproduce in a mechanical form large enough to carry a useful load. The nearest thing to a working device, an ornithopter, is a small, windup children's toy that can stay in the air for several minutes.

ENGRAVING OF A CAYLEY GLIDER

SIR GEORGE CAYLEY

Sir George Cayley (1773–1857) was the first man to understand the basics of winged flight. In the 19th century he built many gliders using these principles. No pilot himself, he once ordered a servant to fly a full-size model. The trip was so hair-raising, the man later resigned.

Pilot held in a strong leather harness

Wing leading edge made of wood

Batlike trailing edges

LEONARDO'S MACHINE

The famous engineer and artist Leonardo da Vinci (1452–1519) conceived various flying machines, including this batlike, flapping device. This full-sized model is based on drawings he made, but is far too heavy – nearly 650 lb (300 kg) – to fly.

Wings attached to main frame

Wings pulled up by ropes worked by hand

Pushing on leg pedals thrusts down wings

FIRST FLIGHTS

THE FIRST EXPERIENCED PILOT was the German Otto Lilienthal. In the 1890s, he built a series of fragile gliders in which he proved many basic principles of controlled flight. After making thousands of flights, he died following a crash in 1896. Seven years later, the Wright brothers made the first controlled flight in a powered machine.

Pilot supported himself on forearms

Wooden spars keep wing in shape

Wings covered with unvarnished cotton

GLIDING ACE
The gliders built by Lilienthal had wooden frames covered with unvarnished cotton, and no moving parts. Lilienthal controlled direction by shifting his body and legs. He made over 2,500 flights before his tragic death in 1896.

FLYER FACTS

• The Wright brothers designed and built the *Flyer* engine.

• The Wright *Flyer's* first flight covered about 120 ft (37 m).

• *Flyer* had a "canard" design: its elevator was in the nose, not the tail.

FRONT VIEW OF WRIGHT FLYER, 1903

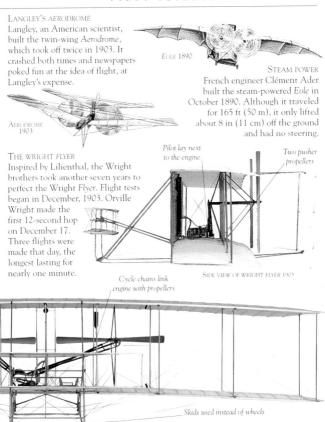

LANGLEY'S *AERODROME*
Langley, an American scientist, built the twin-wing *Aerodrome*, which took off twice in 1903. It crashed both times and newspapers poked fun at the idea of flight, at Langley's expense.

EOLE 1890

AERODROME 1903

STEAM POWER
French engineer Clément Ader built the steam-powered *Eole* in October 1890. Although it traveled for 165 ft (50 m), it only lifted about 8 in (11 cm) off the ground and had no steering.

THE WRIGHT *FLYER*
Inspired by Lilienthal, the Wright brothers took another seven years to perfect the Wright *Flyer*. Flight tests began in December, 1903. Orville Wright made the first 12-second hop on December 17. Three flights were made that day, the longest lasting for nearly one minute.

Pilot lay next to the engine

Two pusher propellers

Cycle chains link engine with propellers

SIDE VIEW OF WRIGHT FLYER 1903

Skids used instead of wheels

EARLY AVIATORS

WITH THE WRIGHT BROTHERS leading
the way, the world went air-crazy.
Within a few years, pioneer aviators in the
US and Europe were tackling the problems of
sustained flight with great success. Experimentation
was the order of the day and some of the results were
bizarre – the Philips Multiplane, for example, had
wings that looked like Venetian blinds.

CURTISS MODEL-D PUSHER
Produced in the US in 1911,
the Model-D had a tricycle
landing gear, forerunner of
the type used in most
aircraft today. Two
years before, Glenn
Curtiss won two
speed events in
his *Golden
Flier* at the
first air show.

*Tailplane carried on
end of wooden
framework*

CHANNEL CROSSING
On July 25, 1909, Louis
Blériot became the first
man to cross the English
Channel. Setting off from Calais,
he flew 23.5 miles (38 km) and touched
down in Dover a celebrity.

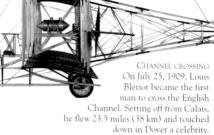

AVIATOR FACTS
• For flying across the
Channel, Blériot won a
cash prize of £1,000.

• The first woman to fly
an aircraft was Thérèse
Péltier in 1908.

• The first seaplane was
built by Frenchman
Henri Fabre in 1910.

BLÉRIOT TYPE XI
Frenchman Louis Blériot's Type XI was a monoplane design, powered by an Anzani motor. Roll control was by bending the trailing edges of the wings ("wing-warping").

Wing covered with stretched linen

BLÉRIOT TYPE XI

EARLY FLYING DRESS

Sheepskin-lined gloves protect hands from frostbite

Leather helmet

Goggles for eye protection

KEEPING WARM
Flying in an early aircraft could be a very cold experience. Where clothing was concerned, thick leather with warm fleece lining was preferred. Later, silks and fur-lined waxed cotton fabric became popular.

Jacket with fold-up collar

Leather boots

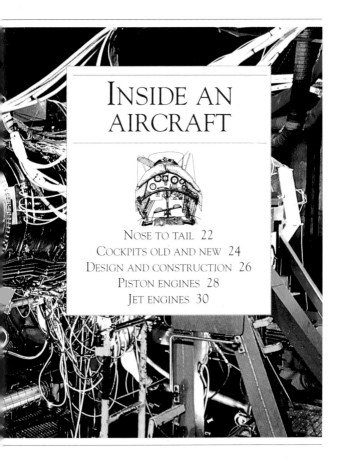

INSIDE AN AIRCRAFT

NOSE TO TAIL

MOST AIRCRAFT SHARE similar details. The main body is called the fuselage, which is slim and sleek in a fighter, or large enough to carry people and freight in an airliner. Wings may be straight for slow speeds, or swept back for faster flight. Some aircraft have swing-wings, which are straight for high lift at slow speed during takeoff, then fold back for high-speed flight.

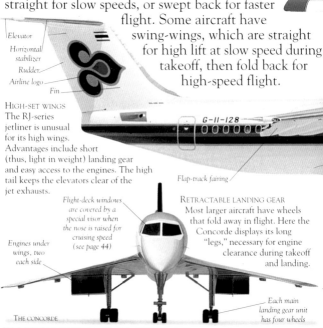

Elevator

Horizontal stabilizer

Rudder

Airline logo

Fin

G-II-128

HIGH-SET WINGS
The RJ-series jetliner is unusual for its high wings. Advantages include short (thus, light in weight) landing gear and easy access to the engines. The high tail keeps the elevators clear of the jet exhausts.

Flap-track fairing

Flight-deck windows are covered by a special visor when the nose is raised for cruising speed (see page 44)

RETRACTABLE LANDING GEAR
Most larger aircraft have wheels that fold away in flight. Here the Concorde displays its long "legs," necessary for engine clearance during takeoff and landing.

Engines under wings, two each side

THE CONCORDE

Each main landing gear unit has four wheels

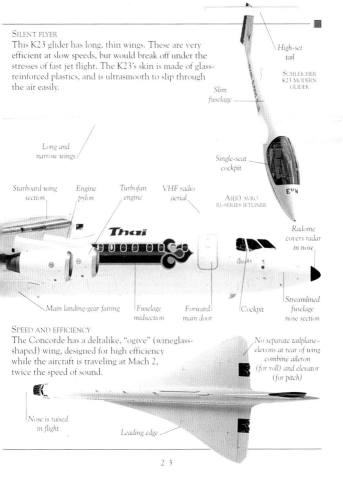

SILENT FLYER
This K23 glider has long, thin wings. These are very efficient at slow speeds, but would break off under the stresses of fast jet flight. The K23's skin is made of glass-reinforced plastics, and is ultrasmooth to slip through the air easily.

High-set tail

SCHLEICHER K23 MODERN GLIDER

Slim fuselage

Long and narrow wings

Single-seat cockpit

AI(R) AVRO RJ-SERIES JETLINER

Starboard wing section

Engine pylon

Turbofan engine

VHF radio aerial

Thai

Radome covers radar in nose

Main landing-gear fairing

Fuselage midsection

Forward main door

Cockpit

Streamlined fuselage nose section

SPEED AND EFFICIENCY
The Concorde has a deltalike, "ogive" (wineglass-shaped) wing, designed for high efficiency while the aircraft is traveling at Mach 2, twice the speed of sound.

No separate tailplane–elevons at rear of wing combine aileron (for roll) and elevator (for pitch)

Nose is raised in flight

Leading edge

COCKPITS OLD AND NEW

THE COCKPIT IS AN AIRCRAFT'S CONTROL CENTER.
The crew has an array of instruments that provides
vital information, and the pilot
controls the machine's direction
using the flight controls. Old and
new cockpits may look different,
but their basic
controls have
changed little
since the
pioneering
days.

EXPOSED TO THE ELEMENTS
The 1911 Avro Triplane is a
single seater with an open
cockpit. In training the
instructor would sit on the wing.

TANDEM SEAT TRAINER
The Tucano is a state-of-the-art, propeller
powered, 1990s combat trainer, with twin
cockpits, each built to resemble a jet fighter.
The instructor sits in the raised rear seat and
can see over the student's head.

FRENCH
SINGLE-
SEATER

Fuel tank
in front
of cockpit

Control
wheel

Rudder
pedals

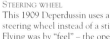

STEERING WHEEL
This 1909 Deperdussin uses a
steering wheel instead of a stick.
Flying was by "feel" – the open
cockpit has no instruments, not
even an airspeed indicator. At the
pilot's feet are rudder pedals to
control "yaw" (sideways motion).

FLYING BY COMPUTER
Modern aircraft have computer-controlled instruments. This Airbus jetliner has fully digital flight controls, with pressure sensors and electronics replacing cable connections.

The A320 has a flight crew of two: a captain and copilot

AIRBUS A320

JETLINER FLIGHT DECK
This array of instruments is the "glass cockpit" of an Airbus A320. Out of sight in this view are the sidestick controllers, one each for the captain (left) and copilot, fixed to either side of the flight deck.

Flight computers controls

Cargo smoke controls

Engine manual start switches

Navigation controls

Radar display

Throttle levers

Rudder pedals and footrests

Systems information displays

A320 FLIGHT DECK

DESIGN AND CONSTRUCTION

THE FIRST AIRCRAFT WERE DESIGNED by trial and error, but within a few years a basic pattern emerged for almost all aircraft. Early aircraft were largely constructed of wood and fabric; today, metal and composite materials are used. The tailplane carries fin, rudder, and elevators. The wings often contain fuel tanks and carry the engines.

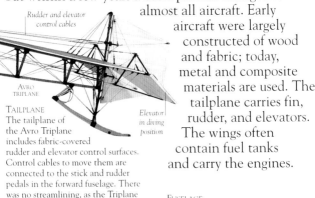

Rudder and elevator control cables

AVRO
TRIPLANE

Elevator in diving position

TAILPLANE

The tailplane of the Avro Triplane includes fabric-covered rudder and elevator control surfaces. Control cables to move them are connected to the stick and rudder pedals in the forward fuselage. There was no streamlining, as the Triplane cruised at a leisurely 45 mph (72 km/h).

FUSELAGE

The 1933 Hawker Hart had a fuselage made of mixed materials. The basic structure is metal tubing in the nose, to take the weight of the engine, with wood for the more lightly loaded rear sections. The whole fuselage is covered with steel sheet, plywood decking, and treated fabric.

Metal engine cradle

Fuel tank

Two cockpits: instructor sat in rear

HAWKER HART TRAINER (1933)

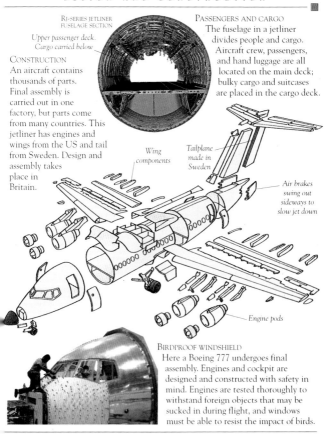

RJ-SERIES JETLINER
FUSELAGE SECTION

Upper passenger deck.
Cargo carried below

CONSTRUCTION
An aircraft contains
thousands of parts.
Final assembly is
carried out in one
factory, but parts come
from many countries. This
jetliner has engines and
wings from the US and tail
from Sweden. Design and
assembly takes
place in
Britain.

PASSENGERS AND CARGO
The fuselage in a jetliner
divides people and cargo.
Aircraft crew, passengers,
and hand luggage are all
located on the main deck;
bulky cargo and suitcases
are placed in the cargo deck.

Wing
components

Tailplane
made in
Sweden

Air brakes
swing out
sideways to
slow jet down

Engine pods

BIRDPROOF WINDSHIELD
Here a Boeing 777 undergoes final
assembly. Engines and cockpit are
designed and constructed with safety in
mind. Engines are tested thoroughly to
withstand foreign objects that may be
sucked in during flight, and windows
must be able to resist the impact of birds.

PISTON ENGINES

APART FROM SOME early steam experiments, all aircraft were powered by piston engines until the arrival of jet power. As in an automobile, an aircraft piston engine explodes fuel in cylinders to drive pistons up and down. This motion is then transferred, via cranks and gears to the propeller, which spins around to move the aircraft forward.

LE RHONE (1914)
Rotary engines had cylinders arranged around the crankshaft. The cylinders spun around to turn the propeller. The twisting (torque) force of high-powered rotaries caused problems in lightweight fighters. These were replaced by cylinders in an in-line or a "V"-arrangement.

BIPLANE SURVIVOR
The Antonov An–2 is the oldest piston-engined biplane in production. Although its first flight was in 1947, it is still made in China as the Harbin Y–5 all-purpose machine.

PROPELLERS
As aircraft evolved, so did propellers. Early props were made of wood; today's are made of steel or complex, carbon-fiber laminated materials. Variable-pitch propellers can be set for the different needs of flight.

PHILLIPS 1893

Spark plugs

Cylinder heads

Cylinder barrels with pistons inside

THREE-CYLINDER ENGINE (DISMANTLED)

Gearbox

Exhaust manifold

Crankshaft

THREE-CYLINDER ENGINE
Using the same principles as early aircraft engines, a modern piston motor uses state-of-the-art design and manufacturing to produce greater reliability. It has far more power, weight for weight, than earlier types.

HIGH-TECH AEROBATICS
The Extra 300 is powered by a tuned, 300-hp six-cylinder Lycoming engine, and is often used for aerobatic displays.

WRIGHT 1909

PARAGON 1909

WOTAN 1917

INTEGRALE 1919

FAIREY-REED 1922

LANG 1917

Steel blade swivels to correct angle during flight

HELE-SHAW-BEACHAM 1928

JET ENGINES

A JET ENGINE is based on simple principles. Air is sucked in and compressed through turbine blades, mixed with a spray of fuel, and ignited. The roaring flame squirts out of the rear nozzle, and pushes the engine forward. There is no vibration from cylinder movement, so a jet is very smooth.

GLOSTER-
WHITTLE
E28/39

This early jet first flew in 1941

TURBOJET
Although smooth and powerful, turbojets are noisy and use a lot of fuel. Most jetliners use turbofans. The Concorde does not; it has four Olympus turbojets with afterburners for more thrust.

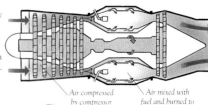

Air compressed by compressor turbine blades

Air mixed with fuel and burned to provide jet thrust

Central engine mounted below fin. Other engines mounted either side

THREE JETS IN THE TAIL
The 1960s Hawker-Siddeley Trident had a trio of engines mounted in the tail section, an arrangement it shared with the Boeing 727. This left the wings clear, and so helped the aerodynamic performance of the plane. Later models of both airliners were equipped with quieter and more economical turbofans.

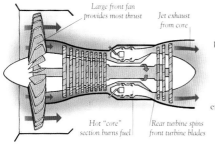

Large front fan provides most thrust

Jet exhaust from core

Hot "core" section burns fuel

Rear turbine spins front turbine blades

TURBOFANS

The turbofan uses a huge, front-mounted fan to provide most of the thrust. Cold air flowing past the hot turbojet "core" masks the high-pitched exhaust shriek. The result is an environment-friendly engine that is much quieter and more economical than a pure turbojet.

AIRBUS A300–600ST

This craft is based on a standard Airbus jetliner. It has been modified for transporting large components between European factories.

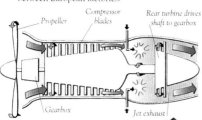

Propeller

Compressor blades

Rear turbine drives shaft to gearbox

Gearbox

Jet exhaust

TURBOPROP

The turboprop uses hot gas exhaust to spin a shaft and propeller via a gearbox. This power plant is suitable for smaller aircraft that do not require high speed – turboprops are quieter and lighter than their piston-engine equivalents.

SWISS TURBOPROP

The single-engine Pilatus PC XII is used as a short-range air taxi and cargo hauler. The aircraft uses "winglets" to smooth the flow of air rolling past the wingtips to save fuel.

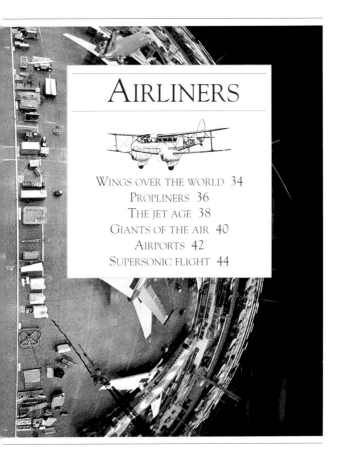

AIRLINERS

WINGS OVER THE WORLD

ON NEW YEAR'S DAY, 1914, Anthony Jannus took off in a two-seater flying boat, carrying the mayor of St. Petersburg, Florida, as his first passenger. The flight across Tampa Bay took just 23 minutes. From this humble beginning the worldwide airline industry was born.

FLYING BOATS OVER THE MEDITERRANEAN
Imperial Airways used a 1931 four-engined Short Kent for the Mediterranean section of its London-India service. The aircraft could carry 15 passengers. It had an advanced metal hull, and suffered no mechanical breakdowns in its first year of service.

Equipment includes auto-pilot – an advanced feature at the time

ADVANCED AIRLINER
The 1933 Boeing Model 247 had many innovative features, including retractable landing gear, a monoplane wing, and a streamlined fuselage. Carrying two pilots, ten passengers, and an air hostess, the 247 could cruise at 170 mph (275 km/h).

Metal fuselage insulated against noise and cold

Pressure tube for airspeed indicator

BASIC AIRLINER

This picture shows the passenger cabin of the de Havilland Dragon, a small eight-passenger biplane airliner of 1933. Accommodation was basic: no heating, no overhead luggage racks, and no in-flight entertainment.

DE HAVILLAND DRAGON CABIN

HANDLEY PAGE HP42

G-AAXD

SLOW BUT SAFE

Claimed to be the "first real airliner," the HP42 had passenger comfort as its main aim. For reduced noise, none of the 38 seats was in line with the engines, and accommodation was luxurious. Cruising speed was only about 100 mph (161 km/h).

BOEING 247D

Pratt and Whitney Wasp radial engine, 550 hp

Main wheels fold into wing, behind engine

Fuel tanks in wings carry a total of 275 gallons (1,036 liters)

BOEING 247 FACTS

• The 247 was the first airliner to have wing and tail deicing equipment.

• Landing speed was a leisurely 59 mph (96 km/h), allowing the use of short airstrips.

PROPLINERS

PROPELLER POWER REIGNED SUPREME through the 1930s and '40s. By the 1950s, the first jetliners were coming into service and the days of the long-range propeller airliner were numbered. Today, propliners are still used, but mainly on short routes that are not busy enough for jets.

ABOVE THE CLOUDS
The 1938 Boeing Stratoliner was the first pressurized airliner, allowing normal breathing at high altitude. The ability to fly high above the troposphere led to an age of smooth and comfortable flight.

TRIPLE-TAIL BEAUTY
The 1950 Lockheed Super Constellation was among the all-time great propeller airliners. It carried 95 passengers across the Atlantic, at 300 mph (483 km/h). Extra fuel for long trips was housed in cigar-shaped tanks at the wingtips.

POPULAR FEEDERLINER
The AI(R) Aero International (Regional) J31 is a 19-seater, often used for "hub and spoke" feeder operations. The "spokes" are air routes linking small airports with a big one, the "hub," and feeding it with passengers for long-distance flights in big jets.

SAAB 2000

This Swedish regional airliner has two turboprops with six-bladed propellers. Turning more slowly than three- or four-blade props, they allow reduced noise from an already quiet design, essential for night-flying to cities.

TURBOPROP ENGINE

This Pratt and Whitney PW120 has features shared by all turboprops. It is basically a jet engine in which thrust is used to spin a propeller, using turbines and a gearbox. Propellers are very efficient up to about 350 mph (564 km/h).

Gearbox

Throttle control

Propeller hub

Air intake

Jet exhaust pipe

DASH-8

The Canadian-made Dash-8, powered by two Pratt and Whitney turboprops, carries up to 56 passengers. It has large flaps, which extend below and behind the wings at takeoff and landing. These allow it to use short airstrips.

Pratt and Whitney PW120 engine

T-tail helps give good control at low speeds

THE JET AGE

THE AGE OF THE JETLINER dawned on May 2, 1952, with the first commercial flight of de Havilland's Comet. The advantages of jet travel were a smooth journey and the aircraft's ability to halve flight times on most routes. Other jets soon entered service, such as the Caravelle, the Boeing 707, and the Douglas DC–8.

DE HAVILLAND COMET
This jet proved popular until a series of accidents, caused by fuselage cracks, spoiled its record. Several years later, the revised Comet 4 (shown here) entered safe airline duty, and a modified version is still flown by the RAF as the Nimrod long-range patrol aircraft.

FINISHING TOUCHES
To ensure an aircraft's strength, all parts are prepared thoroughly with rust-resistant materials. Several coats of corrosion proofing are sprayed on the structure before the airline markings are applied. Engineers then check the aircraft regularly.

Opening cut for forward main door

Bare metal coated in rust-proofer

Radome in nose contains radar antenna

AI(R) AVRO RJ–SERIES PASSENGER JET

Midsection of fuselage

PACKED IN

Seat arrangements vary in different aircraft. This Boeing 777 seat plan shows the two aisles that wide-body jetliners feature. Narrow-bodies, like the RJ-series or Boeing's 737, use just one aisle.

Chair design from the 1950s

SITTING BACK

Seat design has come a long way since the 1920s wicker chairs. Latest types recline and are more comfortable for sleeping.

DIFFERENT VERSIONS

Jetliners come in various sizes: here, the four RJ series models fly together. Basic models can be made longer (to carry more passengers) by adding fuselage sections, and vice versa. Components, such as engines, are adapted to meet the "new" model's requirements.

High-mounted wings attach to center section

Apertures cut ready for portholes in main cabin

Main landing gear folds into lower fuselage bay

Main deck level; cargo is carried underneath in pallets

GIANTS OF THE AIR

JETLINERS INITIATED AN AIR TRAVEL
boom that continues today. Reliable
and economical engine design has been a
key factor in making air travel popular and
cheap. A jetliner is expensive – $130 million-plus
for a Boeing 747 – yet the travel cost per seat is
comparable to that of a car.

*One turbofan
engine on either
side of the tail*

MD90
TWIN-JET

*All-electronic
instruments installed
on flight deck*

STRETCHED JET
The McDonnell Douglas MD90
twin jet may be the most modified
airliner ever produced. The
original DC-9 first flew in 1965.
Since then, the jet has been successfully
stretched, shortened, and reequipped.

BEST SELLER
The smallest Boeing jet, the 737, is
also its best seller. Over 3,500 of these
short-to-medium-range aircraft have been
sold. For a twin jet, the 737 has a fairly
spacious cabin. This is because it uses
the fuselage section of the older, but
larger, 707.

747 FACTS
• The Boeing 747
contains about
4.5 million parts.

• The longest nonstop
747 route, Hong Kong
to Chicago, is 16 hours.

• The amount of paint
on a jumbo jet weighs
more than a horse.

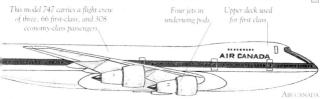

This model 747 carries a flight crew of three, 66 first-class, and 308 economy-class passengers.

Four jets in underwing pods

Upper deck used for first class

AIR CANADA
BOEING 747

BIGGEST JETLINER

When the Boeing 747 first flew in 1969, it was vastly larger than any other jet. Many airports had to be redesigned to cope with the flood of passengers – over 400 at a time – that resulted from the arrival of this jumbo jet.

CREATURE COMFORTS

The latest jetliners include various features to make traveling easier: overhead luggage bins are becoming more spacious; aircraft speed and position is often shown on a moving map display; seat-back TV sets help to alleviate boredom.

INTERIOR OF
BOEING 767

OLD AND NEW

The 1933 Boeing 247D was a leading design of its day, with a smaller, streamlined, all-metal design. It could carry ten passengers at a cruising speed of 170 mph (274 km/h). The 777 is Boeing's latest jet, carrying up to 440 passengers at 582 mph (937 km/h).

AIRPORTS

THE FIRST AIRPORTS were grass airstrips with a few terminal buildings and hangars. Today, major airports are as big as medium-sized towns and employ thousands of workers, from cleaning staff to air traffic controllers. Emergency crews train for accidents, such as a heavy landing or an overrun on takeoff.

EARLIEST ARRIVAL
The earliest airport, Croydon, near London, opened in 1928. It had innovative terminal buildings and a raised control tower.

SPIRIT OF FLIGHT
For Trans World Airlines, architect Eero Saarinen symbolized the spirit of flight with his soaring design for TWA's terminal at John F. Kennedy Airport in New York. It was built in the 1960s, but its swooping shapes still look modern.

Glass walls give passengers a good view of the jets

CONTROL TOWER

This control tower is the nerve center for operations at London's Heathrow airport. Ground controllers have a commanding view over the runways from the upper windows. On lower floors, operators sit in front of radar screens, making sure that airliners are on course.

Ground controllers work in this area

TERMINAL TENTS

Heathrow opened for business just after World War II. Before buildings were completed, passengers had to use tents. Today, the airport has four terminals that cater to over 50 million people each year.

QUICK TURNAROUND

Jets only make money while flying, so a quick turnaround after landing is essential. Refueling takes about 20 minutes, cabins are cleaned and galleys restocked. Engines, instruments, tires, and brakes are checked while cargo and passengers' luggage is loaded.

JETWAY

Swing-out jetways are often used to connect a terminal building with an airliner door. For passengers, it is quicker and easier than climbing down steps.

SUPERSONIC FLIGHT

THE CONCORDE FIRST FLEW in 1969, yet it is the only supersonic airliner in service. Supersonic jets at first seemed to be the wave of the future, but the jumbo-jet age of cheap travel showed that price was valued more than speed. Today, the Concorde is popular with those willing to pay a high price.

ON THE FLIGHT DECK
The Concorde's flight deck is packed with instruments, with seats for crew. Heat caused by air friction during flight at Mach 2 – about 1,320 mph (2,125 km/h) – is such that the fuselage expands almost 12 in (30 cm) in length.

DROOP NOSE
During takeoff and landing, the Concorde's nose droops down to allow the flight crew a clear view. In flight, a retractable visor slides up to cover the cockpit windshield. Fuel is pumped between tanks to help keep the aircraft balanced in the air.

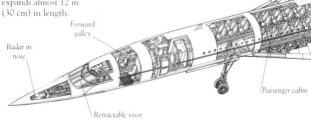

Forward galley

Radar in nose

Retractable visor

Passenger cabin

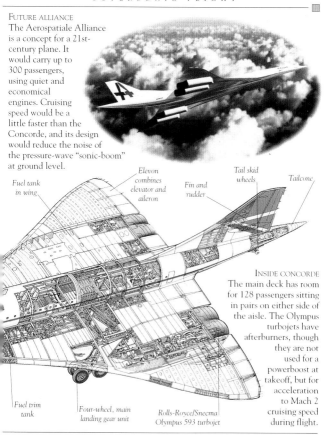

FUTURE ALLIANCE
The Aerospatiale Alliance is a concept for a 21st-century plane. It would carry up to 300 passengers, using quiet and economical engines. Cruising speed would be a little faster than the Concorde, and its design would reduce the noise of the pressure-wave "sonic-boom" at ground level.

Fuel tank in wing

Elevon combines elevator and aileron

Fin and rudder

Tail skid wheels

Tailcone

INSIDE CONCORDE
The main deck has room for 128 passengers sitting in pairs on either side of the aisle. The Olympus turbojets have afterburners, though they are not used for a powerboost at takeoff, but for acceleration to Mach 2 cruising speed during flight.

Fuel trim tank

Four-wheel, main landing gear unit

Rolls-Royce/Snecma Olympus 593 turbojet

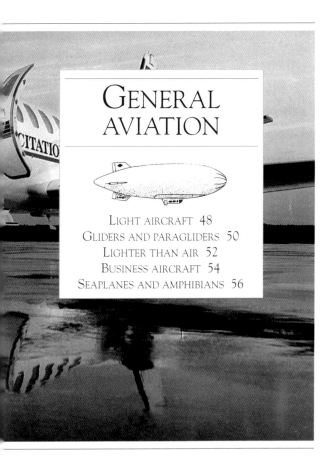

GENERAL AVIATION

LIGHT AIRCRAFT

FOR MANY PEOPLE, learning to fly a single-engine Cessna or Piper at the local flying club is both a thrilling and affordable luxury. Flying an ultralight – typically a design that combines a soft nylon wing with a lightweight seat and engine – is cheaper still. Many are available in kit form for home construction.

MOTH MAGIC
The de Havilland Moth first flew in 1925. The series became the mainstay of club flying the world over. Moths were made in the US, Canada, Britain, and Australia. Many of these aircraft remain in flying condition.

ULTRALIGHTS

TWIN-CYLINDER ENGINE

EXHAUST SYSTEM

PROPELLER

SMALL MACHINE
This ultralight is essentially a powered hang glider. A tiny engine is fixed to the back of a pod, with a propeller that can push the machine along at around 60 mph (97 km/h).

FLIGHT CONTROL
The Pegasus is controlled by moving a metal bar forwards and back, and side to side. A foot throttle changes engine speed. All ultralights have low takeoff and landing speeds, typically about 20 mph (32 km/h).

AEROBATICS
Aerobatic aircraft need to be tough to withstand difficult in-flight maneuvers. The Christen Pitts Special is based on an original 1944 design. The latest version, the Super Stinker, is on order for the US aerobatic team.

DO-IT-YOURSELF FLIGHT
Light aircraft come in various designs; the Snowbird fuselage shown here is typical. The basic structure is made of light but strong aluminum, with engine, wings, and tailplane attached by bolts. Coverings vary, but this design uses plastic film heat-shrunk onto the frame.

Twin-cylinder engine

Tail unit

Fixed landing gear

Airframe made of aluminum

HIGH FLYER
The Cessna Centurion is similar to many other training, pleasure, and business light aircraft. In addition, it boasts a pressurized cabin for high flight, and retractable landing gear for increased speed. The body is all metal.

N7189C

GLIDERS AND PARAGLIDERS

SILENTLY RIDING ON AIR CURRENTS in a glider or paragliding a steerable parachute, attracts thousands of enthusiasts. Early gliders had open cockpits and were fairly inefficient. Today's machines are sleek and streamlined, and use hi-tech materials.

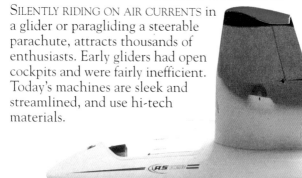

PLASTIC FANTASTIC
This Schleicher K23 is largely made of molded glass-reinforced plastic (GRP). A smooth finish helps to achieve an excellent performance in thermals (rising bubbles of warm air) or in ridge lift (air rising up a hillside).

Tow cable attached to hook under fuselage

Semirecessed mainwheel and nosewheels

PIONEER GLIDER
Octave Chanute built various gliders during the 1890s. More than 1,000 accident-free flights were made on the shores of Lake Michigan.

BUNGEE LAUNCH
"Bungee" launches were popular in the early days, with ground crews hauling on elastic ropes. Today, most launches use a powered winch, winding in a long steel cable.

AERO-TOW

An aero-tow is used to gain more height than is possible from a winch launch. The pilot must concentrate hard, as it is easy to swing off-track behind the tow plane. Once at height, the glider pilot pulls a small handle to release the cable.

Tow plane throttles, glider releases cable

Tow plane and glider climb away from airfield

Oblique lines indicate cable longer than shown

Tow plane uses long cable, hooked onto glider

EVW

CRASH LANDING

Big gliders like the Airspeed Horsa were used in World War II to carry up to 25 fully equipped troops into battle. Landing was sometimes more of a controlled crash – if all aboard survived, it was considered a success.

PARAGLIDING

Paragliders are a combination of both parachute and glider, possessing a glide ratio rivaling that of hang-gliders. Weekend and pilot certificate courses teach beginners to fly solo in as little as one day. It is also possible to fly cross country in a paraglider.

LIGHTER THAN AIR

THE FIRST AVIATORS used the lifting power of hot air or lighter-than-air gases to fly. Today, ballooning is popular all over the world. Airship design, which halted abruptly following the explosion of the Zeppelin *Hindenburg* in 1937, is once again flourishing, and the original Zeppelin company is producing airships at a base at Lake Constance, Germany.

MONTGOLFIER
BALLOON
(1783)

THE MONTGOLFIER BROTHERS
On November 21, 1783, the Montgolfier brothers flew 5 miles (8 km) in their balloon. During the trip, they achieved a maximum height of 3,000 ft (900 m).

SKYSHIP 500HL
AIRSHIP

GO FOR THE BURN
Lifting off in a balloon is a careful procedure. As the air inside gets hotter and gases expand the fabric, the balloon gradually rises. The ground team hangs on to restraining ropes while the crew climbs aboard. Then a continuous burn achieves the final thrust upward into the air.

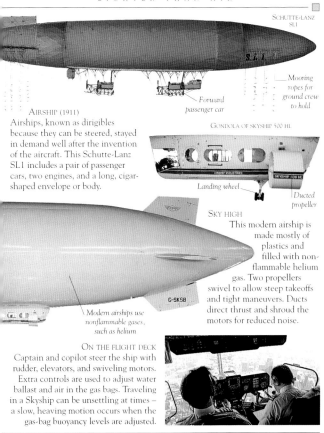

SCHUTTE-LANZ
SL1

S.L.1

*Mooring
ropes for
ground crew
to hold*

*Forward
passenger car*

AIRSHIP (1911)

Airships, known as dirigibles
because they can be steered, stayed
in demand well after the invention
of the aircraft. This Schutte-Lanz
SL1 includes a pair of passenger
cars, two engines, and a long, cigar-
shaped envelope or body.

GONDOLA OF SKYSHIP 500 HL

Landing wheel

*Ducted
propeller*

SKY HIGH

This modern airship is
made mostly of
plastics and
filled with non-
flammable helium
gas. Two propellers
swivel to allow steep takeoffs
and tight maneuvers. Ducts
direct thrust and shroud the
motors for reduced noise.

*Modern airships use
nonflammable gases,
such as helium*

G-SKSB

ON THE FLIGHT DECK

Captain and copilot steer the ship with
rudder, elevators, and swiveling motors.
Extra controls are used to adjust water
ballast and air in the gas bags. Traveling
in a Skyship can be unsettling at times –
a slow, heaving motion occurs when the
gas-bag buoyancy levels are adjusted.

BUSINESS AIRCRAFT

BUSINESS AIRCRAFT RANGE from piston-engined "singles" and "twins" up to sleek jets, such as the Learjet and Challenger. Running costs are high, but top executives value comfort, convenience, and speed. The latest jets have high performance: the 600 mph (966 km/h) Gulfstream GV flies at 51,000 ft (15,555 m) for up to 6,300 miles (10,140 km).

UPTURNED TIPS
The Learjet is regarded as a "sports car" of the business jet world. The upturned wingtips smooth the airflow, adding speed and cutting fuel consumption.

TWIN TURBOPROP
The Super King Air is a widely used business twin. Designed for six executives to sit in comfort, air-taxi King Airs can fit over 13 passengers in smaller seats.
The two Pratt and Whitney turboprops are quiet and reliable.

RAYTHEON LINE-UP
The US Raytheon company produces aircraft ranging from piston engine singles to twin-jet Hawker 1000s. One design is the Starship (above) with pusher propellers, swept wings, and foreplanes ahead of the cockpit.

CHALLENGER 604

The Challenger is one of the largest business jets, with a cabin high enough to stand up straight in. The design was conceived in the 1970s by William Lear of Learjet fame; now Bombardier Canadair manufactures the aircraft.

The 604 is one of the biggest biz-jets available

Upturned wingtips add efficiency

EXECUTIVE INTERIOR

The Challenger has a variety of convenient features: rotating chairs and comfortable sofas, TV, and telephone/fax links are all included. The flight deck is equipped with the latest digital instruments.

LONG HISTORY

The Hawker 800 started out as the de Havilland DH 125, which first flew in 1962. Since then, many of its features have been improved.

CABIN COMFORTS

The Hawker 800's passenger cabin is compact and comfortable, with luxury fittings. The Hawker 1000 is available with more seats. Both have turbofans to cruise quietly at over 40,000 ft (12,200 m).

SEAPLANES AND AMPHIBIANS

THE HEYDAY OF THE FLYING BOAT was the 1920s and 1930s. Transoceanic flights required large aircraft for long-distance flying. Long runways were not available in many places, so a calm stretch of water seemed the obvious answer. The luxurious Empire flying boats of Imperial Airways appeared during this period.

12-ENGINED MONSTER
In 1929, the world's largest plane was the German Dornier Do X, which was capable of carrying 150 people in comfort. It cruised at 118 mph (190 km/h) at 1,640 ft (500 m).

SEAPLANE RACER
The British Supermarine S6B was a seaplane racer that set a world speed record of 340.08 mph (547.3 km/h) in 1931. Three years later, an Italian MC72 raised it to 440.7 mph (709.2 km/h), which lasted for 29 years.

SEA COMFORT
Empire flying boats were introduced in 1936 for mail and passenger flights to Australia, Egypt, Africa, and India. For the 22 passengers, in-flight comforts were ocean-liner standard, with even a promenade section from which to view the passing scenery.

FIRE FIGHTER
The Canadair CL–415, here shown in French civil markings, is specially built for dropping water on forest fires. To refill the tanks, the CL–215 skims along a lake or calm sea, while under-fuselage flaps scoop up water in seconds.

MADE FROM A KIT
The Pétrele biplane is a small, two-seater amphibian from France. Bought in kit form, the aluminum and glass structure takes about 900 hours to build.

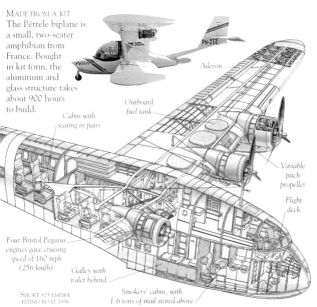

PH-2T2

Aileron

Outboard fuel tank

Cabin with seating in pairs

Variable pitch propeller

Flight deck

Four Bristol Pegasus engines gave cruising speed of 160 mph (256 km/h)

Galley with toilet behind

Smokers' cabin, with 1.6 tons of mail stored above

SHORT S23 EMPIRE
FLYING BOAT 1936

COMBAT AIRCRAFT

AIR SUPERIORITY

THE ULTIMATE REQUIREMENT of air combat is to gain command of the skies, and traditionally the role of fighter aircraft has been vital. Today, hi-tech missiles ensure that many battles take place beyond visual range, though skilled pilots and up-to-date aircraft are still essential for air superiority.

THE BATTLE OF BRITAIN
In 1940, hundreds of aircraft fought for superiority over Britain. British Hurricanes and Spitfires faced German Bf109s and 110s. Dogfights raged at speeds of over 350 mph (563 km/h) around bomber fleets.

SWEPT-WING SURPRISE
Mig–15s were used to deadly effect in the Korean War (1950–3). This Russian-designed jet was faster than the straight-winged American F–80. It was only better trained pilots plus the introduction of the US F–86 Sabre that evened up the balance.

SUPERIOR SUKHOI
The Sukhoi Su–35 is one of the most advanced military jets, boasting a top speed of over Mach 2.3. This twin turbofan Russian aircraft can perform an amazing "cobra" maneuver: it is able to fly backward for a short distance.

F–16
FIGHTING FALCON

The Lockheed Martin F–16 is one of the most popular combat jets. It comes in various forms – fighter, ground-attack, and two-seater – with a top speed of over Mach 2. It is among the cheaper combat jets available: "only" $20 million.

FIGHTER FACTS

• Over 15,000 MiG–15s were made. Some remained in front-line service for 25 years.

• By 1995, 3,500 F–16s had been delivered, with another 400-plus on order.

STEALTHY TOP-GUN
Careful shaping and special materials make the F–22 fighter virtually invisible to radar. Powerful computers and a helmet-mounted sight allow a pilot to select several targets at once.

The F–22 is flying in prototype form at present

The EF2000 can carry at least ten missiles

Foreplanes help the EF2000's maneuverability

EUROFIGHTER 2000

Made by Britain, Germany, Italy, and Spain, the EF2000 is Europe's answer to the SU–35 and F–22. Apart from top performance – the EF2000 goes from zero to Mach 1.5 in under 150 seconds – the aircraft will be one of the most advanced and versatile strike fighters when it enters service.

STRIKE ATTACK

STRIKE-ATTACK AIRCRAFT are crucial in air-to-ground combat. Planes carry a variety of weapons, from anti-radar to runway-buster bombs, and long-range cruise missiles. The Tornado and B–1B swing-wing machines can fly low to avoid enemy radar. The latest Casom cruise missile is designed to be released 300 miles (483 km) from its target.

BIPLANE BOMBER
The Vimy heavy bomber had an ability to carry over a ton of bombs. Later, the Vimy became famous for its long-distance flights, including the first nonstop Atlantic crossing in 1919.

SWING-WING ATTACKER
The Panavia Tornado's wings sweep straight out for takeoff and landing, pulling back to a swept position for high speeds. The basic design comes in antiship, reconnaissance, ground-attack, and long-range air defense types.

Terrain-following radar in nose cone

Navigator/weapons-systems operator (WSO) sits behind pilot

LOW-LEVEL LANCER
The swing-wing Rockwell B–1B Lancer is nearly three times the size of the Tornado. Entering service in the 1980s as the most expensive US military aircraft ever, it cost, an estimated $220 million per plane.

ROCKWELL B–1B LANCER

TANK-BUSTERS

Antitank weapons are designed to penetrate the thickest armor plate. Here a missile is filmed just before impact.

The tank is hit, and a "shaped charge" goes off, blowing a hole in the tank's metal skin with a rocket-like cone of fire.

The tank explodes as the missile's main charge goes off.

Heat exchanger air intake (ram scoop)

Air brake in extended position

Wing in medium-sweep position

Equipment/ weapons installed under fuselage and on wing pylons

WEAPON-LOADED
The Swedish JAS 39 Gripen fighter/ground attacker can carry a huge variety of weapons. Designed to use short runways deep in forests, it can also use adapted roads.

TRANSPORT MACHINES

MORE DOUGLAS DC–3 "Dakotas" from World War II were made than any other transport plane. Known as the C–47 in military service, over 10,000 were made. Today, most cargo aircraft are larger and many are jet-powered.

During the Vietnam War, several C–47s were named "Puff the Magic Dragon" for their firepower

REAR LOADER
Large transport aircraft all feature big rear doors. Not only is it easy to carry outsize loads (such as a helicopter), but it also allows the dropping of parachute cargo during flight. This is achieved by simply pushing prepacked loads straight off the rear ramp.

MIGHTY "HERK"
First flown in 1954, the Hercules has been one of the most widely used transports, with over 30 versions produced. The latest C–130J can haul 40% more cargo, using engines that deliver 29% more thrust while burning 23% less fuel

PROTOTYPE HERCULES 1954

U.S. AIR FORCE

AVIATION LEGEND
The DC–3 began in 1935 as the Douglas Sleeper Transport airliner. As the C–47 in World War II, it fulfilled many roles, acting as glider tug, air ambulance, and paratroop transport.

MIDAIR REFUELING
In-flight refueling is an important job for the air-transport fleet. Here, an RAF Tristar trails a "drogue" fuel hose for the three probe-equipped Jaguars. Once the probe is inserted into the drogue, fuel can be quickly transferred.

REFUELING
JAGUAR ATTACK
AIRCRAFT

PARACHUTE DROP
A C–17 Globemaster III (nicknamed "Moose" for its tall winglets) drops a mixed load. The aircraft can fly up to 2,400 miles (3,864 km), and this can be extended by in-flight refueling. When on the ground, it can use reverse thrust to turn and back into tight spots.

TRANSPORT FACTS
• A fire-fighting Hercules can drop a 2,500-gallon (11,365 liter) waterload in just five seconds.

• The C–17 can lift a 77-ton load off a rough airstrip 7,600 ft (2,316 m) long.

OBSERVATION AND CONTROL

THE FIRST MILITARY AIRCRAFT were World War I spotter planes. Today, early warning of enemy activity is as important, but radar and electronic equipment have replaced simple observation. The crews of command aircraft not only track enemy movements but also control and direct aircraft in response.

The aircraft has a crew rest area in the rear

BIPLANE OBSERVER
The German LVG of World War I had two seats: one for the pilot and one for the observer. Spotting enemy activity was aided by binoculars and sometimes a bulky camera. The LVG also had two machine guns for defense against enemy fighters.

Refueling probe

Radar dish

OBSERVATION FACTS
• The first "sky spy" was an observer in a balloon sent up by the French army in 1794.
• The Italians first used spotter planes against Turkish forces in 1911.

SWEPT-WING SENTRY
Inside the Boeing Sentry sit two pilots, a flight engineer, a navigator – and up to 16 radar operators and controllers. The aircraft's main feature is a huge rotating radar dish on top of the fuselage.

ELECTRONIC EYES
Operators in a command aircraft use computers to receive information about the air, sea, and land below. Once information is gathered, orders can be relayed. Airborne observation posts fly near most of the world's trouble spots.

The Atlantic is the only aircraft specifically designed for antisubmarine and anti-surface warfare

LONG-RANGE PATROL
The Atlantic is used by the French Navy to check on shipping and hunt submarines. Crews use sonobuoys to detect underwater noise, and a magnetic anomaly detector, which detects magnetism caused by a sub's electrical equipment.

UNMANNED SKY SPY
Battlefield skies are dangerous, so an unmanned air vehicle (UAV) is sometimes used instead of a manned aircraft. This camera-equipped Israeli UAV has a small and quiet piston engine.

CARRIER AIRCRAFT

AIRCRAFT CARRIERS CAN QUICKLY DELIVER massive firepower against an enemy. Air operations using ships began in 1861. Observation balloons were towed from a coal barge in the American Civil War. HMS *Argus* was the first "flat-top" carrier in 1918, with 20 torpedo planes.

AIR POWER AT SEA
Torpedo-carrying biplanes became important naval weapons in the 1930s. Such carrier forces were vital in World War II, when air and sea battles raged across the world. Today's biggest carriers can carry over 100 aircraft.

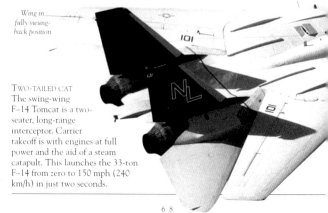

Wing in fully swung-back position

101

NL

101

TWO-TAILED CAT
The swing-wing F–14 Tomcat is a two-seater, long-range interceptor. Carrier takeoff is with engines at full power and the aid of a steam catapult. This launches the 33-ton F–14 from zero to 150 mph (240 km/h) in just two seconds.

Matra Magic heat-seeking missile

Pitch controlled by foreplanes

FRENCH NEWCOMER
Rafale is the latest French multi-role carrier jet, due to fly from the carriers *Foch* and *Clemençeau*. The two-engined machine is a canard design, with foreplanes instead of conventional tail surfaces for pitch control .

HEFTY WEAPON CARRIER
The F/A–18 Hornet, the standard US Navy fighter/attack machine, used by Australia, Canada, and Spain. The "E" version shown here has 11 "hard points" from which to hang bombs, missiles, and fuel tanks.

Radar can guide up to six missiles at once

Command island of aircraft carrier

Maximum speed is about Mach 2.4

Two-seat cockpit

CARRIER TRAINER
The T–45 Goshawk, based on the British Hawk trainer, is adapted for carrier operations. On landing, an arrester hook catches a wire across the deck. This pulls the plane from 140 mph (225 km/h) to a dead stop.

DRESSING FOR COMBAT

IN WORLD WAR I, warm clothing was essential for flying. By World War II, oxygen equipment became necessary for high-altitude flight. Today, military pilots wear clothes to defeat "G" forces – the weight felt as a pilot pulls a tight turn.

Flying helmet with pull-down visor

Oxygen mask

WORLD WAR I COMBAT

READY FOR TAKEOFF
Crew dress in overalls, with anti-G garments and life jacket, oxygen mask, and communications equipment.

Notepad

Line for compressed air

Survival kit pocket

G-FORCE PROTECTION
The G-suit has a compressed air line to prevent blood from pooling in the legs.

FLIGHT LIEUTENANT, BRITISH ROYAL AIR FORCE

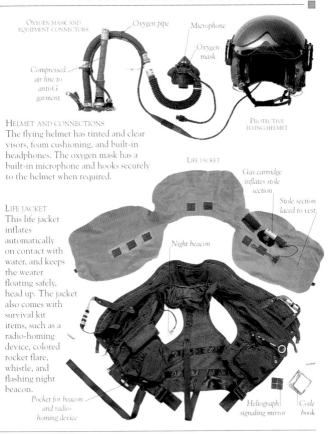

OXYGEN MASK AND
EQUIPMENT CONNECTORS

Oxygen pipe

Microphone

Oxygen
mask

Compressed
air line to
anti-G
garment

PROTECTIVE
FLYING HELMET

HELMET AND CONNECTIONS
The flying helmet has tinted and clear
visors, foam cushioning, and built-in
headphones. The oxygen mask has a
built-in microphone and hooks securely
to the helmet when required.

LIFE JACKET

Gas cartridge
inflates stole
section

Stole section
laced to vest

LIFE JACKET
This life jacket
inflates
automatically
on contact with
water, and keeps
the wearer
floating safely,
head up. The jacket
also comes with
survival kit
items, such as a
radio-homing
device, colored
rocket flare,
whistle, and
flashing night
beacon.

Night beacon

Pocket for beacon
and radio-
homing device

Heliograph
signaling mirror

Code
book

WAR IN
THE AIR

DOGFIGHTS

AERIAL COMBAT IN WORLD WAR I was a deadly affair: the life expectancy of combat pilots could be measured in weeks or days. Cockpit fires were among the greatest hazards. Parachutes were not supplied to the Allies for fear they would encourage cowardice.

Radiator for engine-cooling water

8-cylinder 300 hp Hispano-Suiza "V" engine

Wooden propeller

Solid rubber tires

Fuel tank

BRISTOL F2B FIGHTER

MAN TO MAN
A pilot was counted as an "ace" when he had downed five or more enemy aircraft in combat.

F2B FIGHTER
The F2B (1917) was fast enough to act as both a spotter and fighter aircraft. The conventional design incorporated biplane wings with a wood-frame fuselage and linen covering.

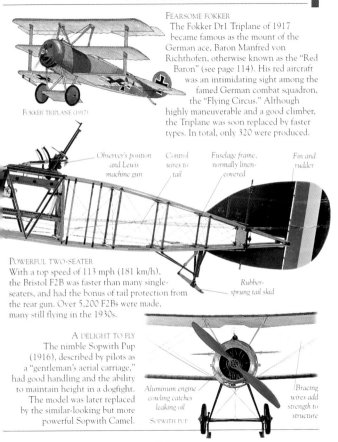

FEARSOME FOKKER

The Fokker Dr1 Triplane of 1917 became famous as the mount of the German ace, Baron Manfred von Richthofen, otherwise known as the "Red Baron" (see page 114). His red aircraft was an intimidating sight among the famed German combat squadron, the "Flying Circus." Although highly maneuverable and a good climber, the Triplane was soon replaced by faster types. In total, only 320 were produced.

FOKKER TRIPLANE (1917)

Observer's position and Lewis machine gun

Control wires to tail

Fuselage frame, normally linen-covered

Fin and rudder

POWERFUL TWO-SEATER

With a top speed of 113 mph (181 km/h), the Bristol F2B was faster than many single-seaters, and had the bonus of tail protection from the rear gun. Over 5,200 F2Bs were made, many still flying in the 1930s.

Rubber-sprung tail skid

A DELIGHT TO FLY

The nimble Sopwith Pup (1916), described by pilots as a "gentleman's aerial carriage," had good handling and the ability to maintain height in a dogfight. The model was later replaced by the similar-looking but more powerful Sopwith Camel.

Aluminum engine cowling catches leaking oil

SOPWITH PUP

Bracing wires add strength to structure

AIR BATTLES

AIRCRAFT DEVELOPMENT ADVANCED in World War II from biplanes to jet fighters capable of nearly 600 mph (966 km/h). The Battle of Britain in 1940 showed that command of the air was crucial to victory on land. In June 1944, Allied air supremacy proved vital to the D-day invasion.

Two 20mm cannon in each wing

SUPERLATIVE SPITFIRES

The tough and maneuverable Spitfire appeared in the skies in 1938. Flying at 355 mph (571 km/h), the fighter was armed with four machine guns in each wing. Over 20,000 were made before production halted in 1947, by which time improvements had enabled the aircraft to reach top speeds of over 450 mph (724 km/h).

"FORKED-TAIL DEVIL"
The P–38 Lightning carried a pilot, four machine guns, and a cannon in the central pod. Supercharged engines gave a speed 410 mph of over (660 km/h). Opposing Japanese flyers nicknamed this aircraft the "forked-tail devil."

TOP SURFACE WING

BOTTOM SURFACE WING

Main landing-gear door

Leading edges of wings painted yellow for ground visibility

All-metal components

Napier Sabre 2,400 hp liquid-cooled engine

Engine exhaust stubs

Aluminum alloy prop blades

PROPELLER

HAWKER TEMPEST
The 1943 Hawker Tempest had advanced features that included a 24-cylinder engine for high speed and climb rate, a "teardrop" canopy for all-around vision, and four powerful cannons in the wings.

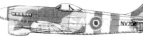

COMPONENTS OF A HAWKER TEMPEST MARK V

V–1 INTERCEPTOR
Among the Tempest's roles was the intercepting of pilotless V–1 "flying bombs." Pilots managed to destroy them by firepower or by tipping their wings over.

RECORD MESSERSCHMITTS
Over 33,000 Messerschmitt 109s were made, the most of any single aircraft type. The 109 was well matched with the Spitfire for speed; it could climb better but not turn as well.

BOMBER RAIDS

THE BOMBERS OF WORLD WAR II ranged from small, fast, and agile types such as the Mosquito, to plodding "bomb trucks" like the Lancaster, which could carry a 22,000 lb (10,000 kg) Grand Slam "earthquake" bomb with enough explosive to flatten a whole city block. In 1945, Japan surrendered after the cities of Hiroshima and Nagasaki were razed to the ground, each by a single atom bomb dropped from a Boeing B–29 Superfortress.

THE "WOODEN WONDER"
Nicknamed for its lightweight, all-wood construction, the twin-engined de Havilland Mosquito of 1940 could cruise at 315 mph (507 km/h), and accelerate to well over 400 mph (644 km/h).

FLYING FORTRESS
The Boeing B–17 was named for its defensive array of up to 14 machine guns. In fact, many B–17s proved to be sitting ducks and were shot down on daylight raids. Fully loaded bombers did not fly much above 200 mph (322 km/h).

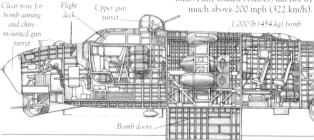

Clear nose for bomb aiming and chin-mounted gun turret

Flight deck

Upper gun turret

1,000 lb (454 kg) bomb

Bomb doors

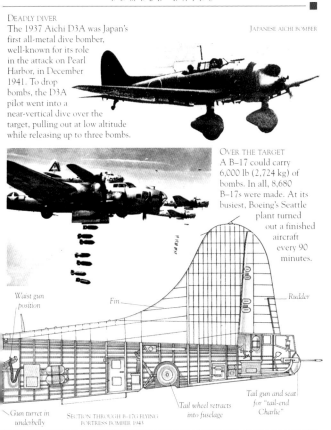

DEADLY DIVER
The 1937 Aichi D3A was Japan's first all-metal dive bomber, well-known for its role in the attack on Pearl Harbor, in December 1941. To drop bombs, the D3A pilot went into a near-vertical dive over the target, pulling out at low altitude while releasing up to three bombs.

JAPANESE AICHI BOMBER

OVER THE TARGET
A B–17 could carry 6,000 lb (2,724 kg) of bombs. In all, 8,680 B–17s were made. At its busiest, Boeing's Seattle plant turned out a finished aircraft every 90 minutes.

Waist gun position

Fin

Rudder

Gun turret in underbelly

Tail wheel retracts into fuselage

Tail gun and seat for "tail-end Charlie"

SECTION THROUGH B–17G FLYING FORTRESS BOMBER 1943

VERTICAL TAKEOFF

HELICOPTER WORLD

ROTARY-WING FLIGHT DAWNED IN 1907 with Paul Cornu's short, hovering liftoff. However, it was not until the 1936 Focke-Wulf Fw 61 that a practical helicopter was developed. Igor Sikorsky's VS–300 of 1940 had a large rotor for lift and a small tail rotor for direction control – a design pattern widely used since.

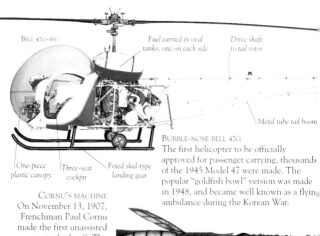

BELL 47G-3B1

Fuel carried in oval tanks, one on each side

Drive shaft to tail rotor

Metal tube tail boom

One-piece plastic canopy

Three-seat cockpit

Fixed skid-type landing gear

BUBBLE-NOSE BELL 47G
The first helicopter to be officially approved for passenger carrying, thousands of the 1945 Model 47 were made. The popular "goldfish bowl" version was made in 1948, and became well known as a flying ambulance during the Korean War.

CORNU'S MACHINE
On November 13, 1907, Frenchman Paul Cornu made the first unassisted vertical takeoff. The 20-second hop barely lifted his twin rotor "flying bicycle" off the ground. Later flights achieved an altitude of 6.5 ft (2 m).

OIL-RIG CARRIER
A Super Puma transports workers to an offshore oil rig. The two engines are a vital safety feature at sea – if one fails, the other has enough power to fly.

SURVIVAL SUITS
On North Sea oil rig flights, all passengers wear specially insulated suits. In case of emergency "ditching" on the open sea, a suit's multilayer material is essential for survival in icy winter waters.

-BGID

Tail rotor for direction control

NO-TAIL ROTOR TECHNOLOGY
The McDonnell Douglas MD–520N uses NOTAR (no tail rotor) technology. Instead of a tail rotor, steering is controlled by a system using turbine exhaust gases.

K-MAX
The Kaman K-Max is a single-seat "flying truck," designed for heavy hauling. Power is generated by two angled rotors that intermesh as they spin – a unique design claimed as efficient and safe.

CHOPPERS INTO BATTLE

THE FIRST MILITARY HELICOPTER, the Sikorsky R–4, was produced in 1944 and soon after made the first helicopter evacuation of an injured soldier. Since then, "choppers" have become famous for their air-rescue abilities, as fighting gunships, and for antisubmarine missions.

SIKORSKY R–4
The R–4 was developed from Sikorsky's experimental VS–300, with which it shared the same type of fabric-covered, steel-tube framework. This helicopter was the first to land on a ship at sea.

Gearbox

Main rotor has three blades

E

Two-seat cabin

Engine housed in central section

ARMED APACHE
The AH-64D Apache has a radar dish above the main rotor mast to track enemy vehicles. Once locked on, the Apache's weapons operator can use radar-guided missiles.

ANGLO-ITALIAN FLYER
The EH101 derives its flying performance from three turbines. This power allows for a multipurpose role, including troop transport, antisubmarine, and as a civil Heliliner.

MIDAIR RESCUE
This British Royal Navy Lynx
is equipped with nose-mounted
weapons-sighting gear to make it
an efficient combat machine. But such
helicopters can be used for other jobs, such
as rescue missions. Here, a stretcher patient is
winched aboard before being taken to the hospital.
Powered by two Rolls-Royce
turboshaft engines, the Lynx
has a maximum cruising speed
of 161 mph (259 km/h).

*Tail rotor is
used to control
flight direction*

*Tail-rotor
pitch-control
wires*

Tail boom

SIKORSKY R-4

KK99S

*Rear landing
wheel*

*Turboprop engine in
each wingtip pod*

*V-22 carries
two crew and
up to 24 troops*

*Wide rear
door for fast
loading*

V-22
OSPREY

Props tilt forward in flight

Props gradually swing upward

V-22 OSPREY
The Bell/Boeing Osprey has tilt-
rotors that allow helicopter-style
operations. Top speed is about
275 mph (443 km/h), one third
faster than most helicopters can fly.

Props tilt up for vertical landing

JET LIFT

THE HARRIER LINE started with the P1127 prototype of 1960, and is the only really successful, vertical takeoff, fixed-wing aircraft. In service, vertical takeoff is rare, as it uses a lot of fuel and allows only a small weapon load to be carried. Usually the plane makes a short takeoff and reserves hovering for vertical landing at the mission's end.

ARMED TO THE TEETH
The Harrier II flown by the US Marine Corps can carry a variety of weapons. Here, outer pylons carry Sidewinder air-to-air missiles, while the inner pylons carry bombs. Guns are also mounted under the fuselage.

Armored bird-proof windshield

In-flight refueling probe in stowed position

HARRIER GR5
The single-seat GR5 is used for battlefield close-support and reconnaissance. Unusually, the Harrier has a fore-aft "bicycle" arrangement for the landing gear, with small outer wheels for balance. The aircraft can be refueled in midair using the fold-out probe situated behind the canopy.

Single front wheel

JET LIFT

THE SECRET OF JET LIFT

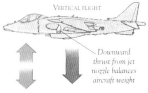

FORWARD FLIGHT

VERTICAL FLIGHT

Jet thrust from rearward-vectored nozzles pushes aircraft forward

Downward thrust from jet nozzle balances aircraft weight

SWIVELING NOZZLES
Four swiveling nozzles are the key to the Harrier's abilities. Pointing back (above), they push the aircraft forward at up to 661 mph (1,064 km/h).

HOVER AND MANEUVER
Pointing straight down, the nozzles enable jet thrust to support the aircraft in midair. Small "puffer" nozzles in wings and tail aid steering.

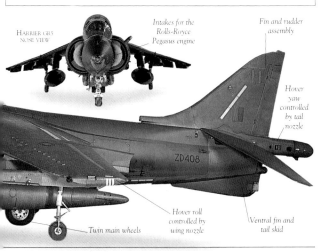

HARRIER GR5 NOSE VIEW

Intakes for the Rolls-Royce Pegasus engine

Fin and rudder assembly

Hover yaw controlled by tail nozzle

ZD408

Hover roll controlled by wing nozzle

Twin main wheels

Ventral fin and tail skid

NAVIGATION AND SAFETY

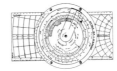

FINDING THE WAY

IN THE EARLY DAYS OF FLYING, commercial pilots followed roads and train tracks. Things changed in 1922 after a mid-air collision by two airliners over northern France. After this, a system of air lanes was devised – captains had to file a flight plan before takeoff, and the aircraft would have to stay in its appointed air lane.

Map kept in waterproof wallet

MAPS
Early pilots had to rely on road maps. Following landmarks was the only way to avoid getting lost.

Rotating metal reflector dish

Mounting system for antenna

Radar normally positioned at the edge of airfield

Equipment housing

RADAR FACTS
• Radar stands for "Radio Direction And Ranging."
• Radar was first developed in Britain in the 1930s.
• The first ground radar was built in 1937 to detect enemy bombers.

RADAR ANTENNA
This 1950s-era antenna was used to keep a radar eye on approaching and departing aircraft. Images from the constantly rotating "dish" are relayed to screens in a control tower, where controllers ensure that all local aircraft are on the correct flight path.

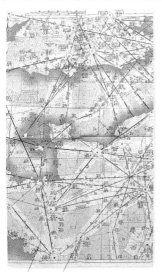

NAVIGATION CHART
Even with the advent of electronic equipment, paper charts are still essential. This navigator's chart includes air lanes (black lines) together with their names and height levels, radio beacons (circles), and compass headings (numbers next to beacon circles).

ARTIFICIAL HORIZON
The "own aircraft" symbol shows if the plane is banking, climbing, or diving. This is essential for accurate flying in clouds.

DIRECTION FINDER
By lining up the "own aircraft" symbol with the white arrow, a pilot can follow the signal from a ground radio beacon.

Air lane

Radio beacon

Groundspeed and airspeed

Cloud storm cells

Track of aircraft

RADAR DISPLAY
This cockpit instrument displays vital information. Colored patches show cloud, with red areas as turbulence. The long line shows the aircraft's track, with current position marked at the bottom. Groundspeed and airspeed are shown at top left, while bearing and distance to the next radio beacon are at top right.

SAFETY EQUIPMENT

FLYING IN AN AIRLINER is one of the safest ways to travel, but on-board safety equipment is essential. First-aid kits are used for minor, in-flight illnesses. Emergency oxygen equipment to cope with cabin-air failure is standard, as are inflatable life jackets and emergency escape slides in the event of a bad landing.

FIRST-AID BOX

Jacket rolls up small enough to fit under seat

OXYGEN EQUIPMENT
In the event of cabin-air loss, emergency oxygen masks automatically drop down from overhead racks. A separate oxygen cylinder is kept to help passengers with breathing difficulties.

OXYGEN MASK

OXYGEN CYLINDER

LIFE JACKET
A life jacket is carried under each seat, rolled up in a neat pack. Cabin crews give demonstrations before takeoff. Every jacket has a compressed gas cylinder for inflation and a top-up nozzle. There is also a whistle and light beacon.

Rolled up jacket

ADULT/CHILD
RFD LIFEJACKET

SK 1

PL1

Megaphone boosts volume of voice

Axe made of strong alloy

MEGAPHONE   ESCAPE AXE   FIRE EXTINGUISHER

EMERGENCY ITEMS
Essential items include an extinguisher for putting out minor fires, and a megaphone used to guide people in an escape. The axe can be used to hack an escape route in case getting out of the aircraft is difficult. Floor lighting is used in the event of a smoke-filled cabin.

ESCAPE SLIDE
Exit is quick via inflatable slides that pop out from doors and emergency exits.

"BLACK BOX" RECORDER
In the event of a crash, flight recorders continuously note all flight details. Many aircraft also have flight-deck voice recorders to give vital clues.

Fireproof box

Magnetic tape equipment

Aircraft systems plug in here

EJECT! EJECT!

THE GERMANS FIRST USED ejection seats in 1941, and over the next four years more than 60 Luftwaffe (German air force) pilots ejected to safety. The original gas-fired systems resulted in many back injuries, but today's seats use rocket power for smoother acceleration. An ejection seat is simple to use – pull the firing handle, the seat bangs out, the parachute opens, and the seat falls away.

ZERO-ZERO EJECTION
Early ejection seats only worked at high altitudes. Today's seats are designed for zero-altitude, zero-height performance – the seat can blast away from a standing aircraft, going high enough for the parachute to open safely.

SURVIVAL EQUIPMENT

Signal mirror and compass

Signal flare

Blanket

Survival vest

Ground-marker panels

Knife

Drinking water container

SURVIVAL EQUIPMENT
Baling out over enemy territory may mean living off the land before rescue is possible. It is vital that combat crews have survival gear to deal with every situation.

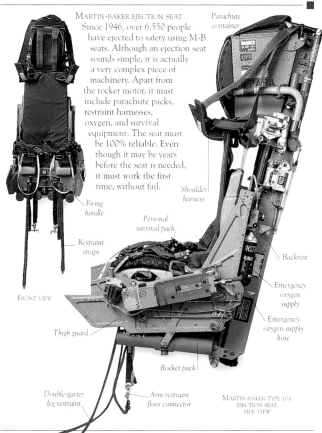

MARTIN-BAKER EJECTION SEAT
Since 1946, over 6,550 people have ejected to safety using M-B seats. Although an ejection seat sounds simple, it is actually a very complex piece of machinery. Apart from the rocket motor, it must include parachute packs, restraint harnesses, oxygen, and survival equipment. The seat must be 100% reliable. Even though it may be years before the seat is needed, it must work the first time, without fail.

Parachute container

Shoulder harness

Firing handle

Restraint straps

Personal survival pack

Backrest

Emergency oxygen supply

Emergency oxygen supply hose

FRONT VIEW

Thigh guard

Rocket pack

Double-garter leg restraint

Arm restraint floor connector

MARTIN-BAKER TYPE 10A
EJECTION SEAT
SIDE VIEW

THE
LEADING EDGE

BELL X–1

X-PLANES

EXPERIMENTAL AIRCRAFT test the frontiers of aviation. The most famous research aircraft is the Bell X–1, flown at supersonic speed by "Chuck" Yeager in 1947. The orange machine was named *Glamorous Glennis* after his wife. Since then, many X-planes have been made, from the bullet-shaped X–15 to the sleek-looking X–31.

FLYING PEBBLE
The HL–10 of 1966 was a wingless "lifting body" single-seater, dropped from a B–52 mother plane. Its flights helped research the shapes for the Space Shuttle.

Fins provide steering control

Lightweight ejection seat

Single-seat cockpit

Clear plastic nose for good landing view

X–15 WITH EXTERNAL TANKS
On October 3, 1967, the X–15A–2 rocket-plane touched Mach 6.73, still the fastest speed by a winged aircraft. X–15s reached altitudes of more than 50 miles (80 km).

HL–10

Air data sensor boom

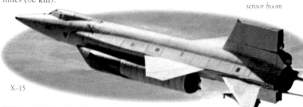

X–15

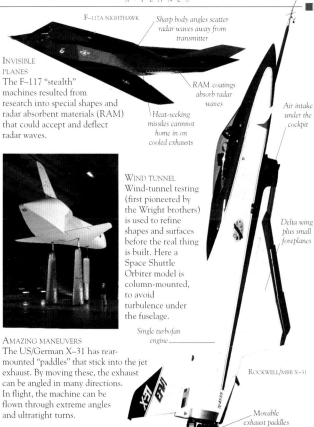

F–117A NIGHTHAWK

Sharp body angles scatter radar waves away from transmitter

INVISIBLE PLANES

The F–117 "stealth" machines resulted from research into special shapes and radar absorbent materials (RAM) that could accept and deflect radar waves.

RAM coatings absorb radar waves

Heat-seeking missiles cannnot home in on cooled exhausts

Air intake under the cockpit

Delta wing plus small foreplanes

WIND TUNNEL

Wind-tunnel testing (first pioneered by the Wright brothers) is used to refine shapes and surfaces before the real thing is built. Here a Space Shuttle Orbiter model is column-mounted, to avoid turbulence under the fuselage.

Single turbofan engine

AMAZING MANEUVERS

The US/German X–31 has rear-mounted "paddles" that stick into the jet exhaust. By moving these, the exhaust can be angled in many directions. In flight, the machine can be flown through extreme angles and ultratight turns.

ROCKWELL/MBB X–31

Movable exhaust paddles

ELECTRONIC REVOLUTION

THE MOST IMPORTANT IMPROVEMENT in today's aircraft concerns their electronic systems. The use of computerized instrument displays and digital engine control has increased reliability and safety. Computer flight simulators can be used to train pilots before they even step into the cockpit of a real plane.

COMPUTER CONTROL
In most new aircraft, lightning-quick computer reflexes control almost all the flying. The flight crew's job is to monitor progress and check the on-board systems.

B–2 STEALTH BOMBER

FLY-BY-WIRE
All new Airbus jets feature FBW controls, in which electronic signals link the cockpit controls with the ailerons, elevators, and rudder.

FLIGHT SIMULATOR
Flight crews can practice for all kinds of challenging emergencies that would be too difficult or dangerous to do in a real aircraft.

ELECTRONIC ENTERTAINMENT
Many airlines offer passengers movies
on seat-back TV screens as well as
digital hi-fi sound. Telephones are also
popular for in-flight use.

SMALLER AND SMALLER
As far as enemy radar is concerned, the
huge B–2 appears little larger than a
seagull. RAM coatings made of secret
carbon/graphite mixtures scatter radar
energy away from enemy receivers.

SAFER DOGFIGHTING
Simulators train military pilots for deadly
combat situations where lives – and
highly expensive fighters – are at stake.

FUTURE FLYERS

TOMORROW'S AIRCRAFT are being test-flown or are at the planning stages. Airbus Industrie's giant A3XX will compete with the Boeing 747. Clean-burning new fuels, such as liquid hydrogen, are being tested. A new generation of fighters will replace existing aircraft, and spaceplanes will supersede the Space Shuttle.

AIRBUS A3XX

DOUBLE-DECK AIR GIANT

The A3XX will be a competitor to Boeing's 747 "jumbo jet." It will be a huge aircraft with two decks for passengers, and cargo on the bottom. Some cargo bays may be modified as luxury sleeping compartments.

Four turbofan engines

STEALTH HELICOPTER

The Boeing Sikorsky Comanche is tomorrow's two-seat combat chopper. When used as a low-level scout, weapons can be stored inside, ensuring that the machine's body stays smooth and "stealthy." A gun turret is mounted under the nose.

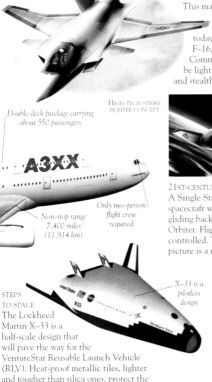

WINGS OF THE FUTURE

This may be the shape of wings to come, a strike fighter that could replace several of today's aircraft including the F–16, Harrier, and Jaguar. Common to all versions will be light weight, high agility, and stealth features.

HIGH-TECH STRIKE FIGHTER CONCEPT

Double-deck fuselage carrying about 550 passengers

A3XX

Non-stop range 7,400 miles (11,914 km)

Only two-person flight crew required

21ST-CENTURY SPACECRAFT

A Single Stage To Orbit (SSTO) spacecraft will take off vertically, gliding back like today's Shuttle Orbiter. Flights will be fully computer-controlled. The engine shown in this picture is a new "aerospike" design.

STEPS TO SPACE

The Lockheed Martin X–33 is a half-scale design that will pave the way for the VentureStar Reusable Launch Vehicle (RLV). Heat-proof metallic tiles, lighter and tougher than silica ones, protect the body. The first flight is due in March 1999.

X–33 is a pilotless design

FUTURE FACTS

• New 747s to compete with the A3XX will seat 462–548 passengers.

• The landing gear will have 20 wheels.

• A proposed DC–X SSTO spacecraft may use an aircraft carrier as a mobile launch pad.

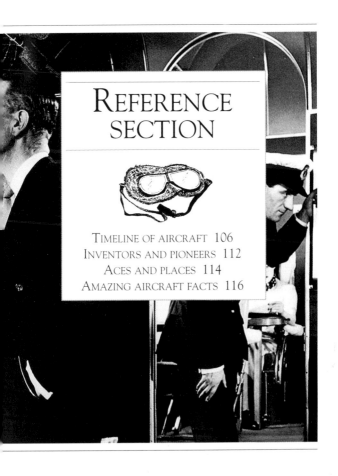

REFERENCE
SECTION

TIMELINE OF AIRCRAFT

AIRCRAFT HAVE AFFECTED OUR LIVES immensely, in both peace and war. Until the 1970s, aircraft design focused mainly on increased speed. Today, computer-aided design and advanced electronics aim at producing greater reliability and fuel economy.

	1300	1874	1890	1903
LANDMARKS OF FLIGHT	• 1300 Marco Polo sees man-carrying kites in China. • 1783 First flight of the Montgolfier hot-air balloon. • 1850s Sir George Cayley begins gliding experiments in England. • 1857 Felix du Temple de la Croix builds a clockwork model aircraft.	• 1874 Felix du Temple's steam-powered craft takes off briefly. • 1884 Russian Alexander Mozhaiski's monoplane makes a short flight. • 1890 Clément Ader of France, makes a brief flight in the steam-powered *Eole*.	LILIENTHAL GLIDER • 1890s Otto Lilienthal test-flies hang gliders. • 1894 Australian Lawrence Hargrave leaves the ground in his box kite. • 1897 Three Swedes die in a balloon attempt to fly over the North Pole.	• 1903 Charles M. Manley crashes Samuel Langley's *Aerodrome* into the Potomac. • 1903 Wright brothers make the first successful flights in a powered aircraft at Kitty Hawk. WRIGHT FLYER
TRANSPORTATION MILESTONES	• 1850s Railway networks expand. • 1856 English scientist Henry Bessemer devises cheap way to make steel.	• 1860s First experimental car built by Austrian Siegfried Marcus. • 1863 First underground railway, London.	• 1881 First all-steel cargo ship, *Servia* in Britain. • 1895 First main-line electric railway in US.	• 1901 Electric trams used in Britain. • 1901 Commercial monorail built in Germany.

	1906	1908	1912	1914
LANDMARKS OF FLIGHT	• 1906 Brazilian Alberto Santos Dumont in his 14-bis "tail-first" biplane is the first man to fly in Europe. • 1907 French Gyroplane No.1 is the first helicopter to lift off with a pilot on board. CORNU'S HELICOPTER • 1907 Paul Cornu hovers for 20 seconds in his untethered helicopter. Later flights reach about 6.5 ft (2 m) from the ground.	• 1908 Charles Furnas becomes the first air passenger. • 1908 Henry Farman makes first circular flight in Europe. • 1908 Thérèse Péltier becomes the first woman to fly solo. • 1908 British Thomas Selfridge is first fatality from an air crash. • 1909 World's first air show, at Reims, France. • 1909 Louis Blériot flies across the English Channel. BLÉRIOT'S MONOPLANE	• 1912 The Avro F is the first monoplane with enclosed cabin. • 1913 French pilot Roland Garros flies the Mediterranean Sea by air. • 1913 Igor Sikorsky's four-engined *Russkiy Vitiaz* ("Russian Knight") is the first successful big aircraft. • 1913 Earliest aerial combat, in the form of pistol shots, takes place during Mexican Civil War.	• 1914 World's first airline opens in Florida, flying across Tampa Bay in a Benoist flying boat. • 1914 First air attack on a city: Paris is bombed. • 1914 First plane shot down. Frenchman Louis Quenault shoots down a German Aviatik in a dogfight over the Western Front, France. • 1915 Dutch designer Anthony Fokker devises a control to allow an aircraft's guns to fire forward, between the spinning propeller blades.
TRANSPORTATION MILESTONES	• 1901 Werner brothers design motorcycle. • 1905 Motor buses replace horse-drawn buses, US.	• 1908 Ford Model T car first sold in US. • 1912 *Titanic*, the largest-ever "unsinkable" ocean liner sinks.	• 1912 First Harley Davidson motorcycle, US. • 1914 Panama Canal opens. • 1916 Tanks developed by	British and French. • 1917 Destroyer ships used in World War I, carrying torpedos.

1918	1919	1926	1928
•1918 The "Red Baron" (von Richthofen), Germany's top fighter ace, is killed in action. •1919 First daily passenger service, between Weimar and Berlin, Germany. •1919 First transatlantic flight, made by a US Navy NC-4 flying boat. •1919 The Junkers F-13 is the first multi-seat, all-metal airplane in commercial use.	•1919 First non-stop transatlantic flight, by Britons Alcock and Brown, in a Vickers Vimy. •1919 KLM, the oldest airline still flying under the same name, is established. •1922 First midair collision involves two airliners flying between London and Paris. Air lane system devised as a result. •1924 Douglas World Cruisers make first flight around the world.	•1926 Americans Richard Byrd and Floyd Bennett fly over the North Pole in a Fokker FVII/3m. Shortly after, Italian Umberto Nobile follows in the *Norge* airship. SPIRIT OF ST. LOUIS •1927 Charles Lindbergh makes first solo non-stop transatlantic flight in *Spirit of St. Louis*. The distance covered was 3,610 miles (5,810 km) in 33½ hours.	•1928 Australian Charles Kingsford-Smith and his crew make the first flight across the Pacific Ocean. •1929 Dornier Do X giant flying boat makes its maiden voyage. •1929 Bernt Balchen and Richard Byrd, in a Ford Trimotor, make first flight over the South Pole. •1930 Amy Johnson is first woman to fly solo from England to Australia. •1933 Boeing 247 makes its first flight.
(LANDMARKS OF FLIGHT) JUNKERS F-13			
•1921 Model A, Duesenberg is first car with hydraulic brakes. •1923 First diesel truck by Benz company.	•1924 Tankers used to transport crude oil. •1929 Five million new cars sold in US.	•1930 Steam tugs first used in Britain. •1935 Sports cars become popular in US.	•1932 Sydney Harbour Bridge opens. •1936 German U-boats very effective during World War II.

	1933	1937	1939	1944
LANDMARKS OF FLIGHT	•1933 First solo around-the-world flight, by American pilot Wiley Post, in a Lockheed Vega *Winnie Mae*. •1933 First flight over Mt. Everest. •1935 Douglas DC–3 first flight. Goes on to be most successful air transport ever made. DOUGLAS DC–3 •1937 Hanna Reich test-flies the first fully controllable helicopter, the Focke-Achgelis Fw61.	•1937 Amelia Earhart, the first woman to cross the Atlantic, disappears over the Pacific Ocean. •1937 Zeppelin *Hindenburg* crashes in flames at Lakehurst, New Jersey. •1938 Boeing Stratoliner, the first airliner with pressurized cabin, makes first flight. •1939 Boeing Clipper flying boat used for regular North Atlantic airmail service.	•1939 First flight by a jet-propelled aircraft, the German-built Heinkel He 178. •1939 World War II begins as German aircraft fly into Poland. •1940 Igor Sikorsky's VS–300 helicopter takes off; his main and tail rotor design is still used. •1940 Battle of Britain. •1941 Italian Fiat CR 42B flies at 323 mph (520 km/h), a biplane world record that still stands.	ME 262 •1944 Messerschmitt Me 262 is world's first operational jet fighter. •1944 First all-jet combat. British Gloster Meteor destroys a V–1 flying bomb by tipping its wingtip over. •1945 Boeing B–29s drop two atomic bombs on Hiroshima and Nagasaki, ending the war in the Pacific theater. •1947 Chuck Yeager breaks the sound barrier in the Bell X–1.
TRANSPORTATION MILESTONES	•1937 Golden Gate Bridge opens in San Francisco. •1939 German battleships are replaced by	aircraft carrier; at end of World War II. •1941 Cargo steamer Liberty ships mass-produced in US.	•1941 Largest ever steam locomotives haul huge freight loads in US. •1944 "Jeeps" used by US army.	•1946 Aircraft carriers change the nature of sea warfare as aircaft can attack targets beyond warship guns.

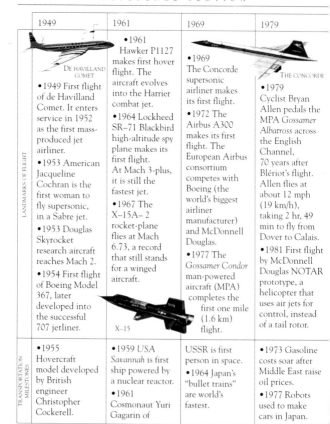

1949	1961	1969	1979

LANDMARKS OF FLIGHT

DE HAVILLAND COMET

- 1949 First flight of de Havilland Comet. It enters service in 1952 as the first mass-produced jet airliner.
- 1953 American Jacqueline Cochran is the first woman to fly supersonic, in a Sabre jet.
- 1953 Douglas Skyrocket research aircraft reaches Mach 2.
- 1954 First flight of Boeing Model 367, later developed into the successful 707 jetliner.

- 1961 Hawker P1127 makes first hover flight. The aircraft evolves into the Harrier combat jet.
- 1964 Lockheed SR-71 Blackbird high-altitude spy plane makes its first flight. At Mach 3-plus, it is still the fastest jet.
- 1967 The X-15A-2 rocket-plane flies at Mach 6.73, a record that still stands for a winged aircraft.

X-15

- 1969 The Concorde supersonic airliner makes its first flight.
- 1972 The Airbus A300 makes its first flight. The European Airbus consortium competes with Boeing (the world's biggest airliner manufacturer) and McDonnell Douglas.
- 1977 The Gossamer Condor man-powered aircraft (MPA) completes the first one mile (1.6 km) flight.

THE CONCORDE

- 1979 Cyclist Bryan Allen pedals the MPA Gossamer Albatross across the English Channel, 70 years after Blériot's flight. Allen flies at about 12 mph (19 km/h), taking 2 hr, 49 min to fly from Dover to Calais.
- 1981 First flight by McDonnell Douglas NOTAR prototype, a helicopter that uses air jets for control, instead of a tail rotor.

TRANSPORTATION MILESTONES

- 1955 Hovercraft model developed by British engineer Christopher Cockerell.

- 1959 USA Savannah is first ship powered by a nuclear reactor.
- 1961 Cosmonaut Yuri Gagarin of

USSR is first person in space.
- 1964 Japan's "bullet trains" are world's fastest.

- 1973 Gasoline costs soar after Middle East raise oil prices.
- 1977 Robots used to make cars in Japan.

	1986	1993	1994	1996
LANDMARKS OF FLIGHT	• 1986 Rutan *Voyager* makes the first non-stop, unrefueled flight around the world, piloted by Dick Rutan and Jeana Yeager. The trip covers 25,012 miles (40,252 km) and takes nine days. F–117A • 1991 Lockheed F–117A flies combat missions in the Gulf War. Designed to absorb or deflect enemy radar, it is the first "stealth" aircraft to see action.	• 1993 First flight of the Airbus A321, a longer version of the A320, the world's first fly-by-wire airliner, in which electronic signals replace the usual control cables. • 1994 First flight of the Boeing 777 twin jet. • 1994 Eurofighter EF2000 makes first flight. • 1994 Airbus A300–600ST first flies. Its huge cargo hold is big enough to accommodate an entire airliner fuselage.	• 1994 A Boeing 757 makes the world's highest airliner landing, at Tibet's Bangda Airport, 14,219 ft (4,375 m) above sea level. • 1994 Jo Salter becomes the Royal Air Force's first female combat pilot. • 1995 Indonesian N–250 twin turboprop makes its first flight. • 1996 The Concorde sets new transatlantic airline speed record, from New York to London, in 172 min, 59 sec.	• 1996 Five Airbus airliners are fitted with equipment to determine if jet exhausts are polluting the upper atmosphere. • 1996 German Zeppelin company resumes as airship maker, ZLT. • 1996 X–33, American research spacecraft first flight is planned for March 1999. X–33
TRANSPORTATION MILESTONES	• 1981 Space Shuttle *Columbia* first successful orbital flight. • 1992 Japanese invent first ship propelled by	magnetic forces, the *Yamoto*. • 1993 Russia and America agree to work on permanent space station.	• 1993 California law says cars must be emission-free after 2003. • 1994 Channel tunnel rail link opens between	England and France. • 1994 Hong Kong begins world's biggest airport on artificial island.

INVENTORS AND PIONEERS

TODAY, THE DESIGN AND MANUFACTURE of aircraft is a worldwide industry, but in the past it was individuals that counted. The inventors and pioneers shown on these pages are some of the key people who have shaped the course of aircraft development.

OTTO LILIENTHAL (1848–1896)

A German gliding pioneer, Lilienthal made about 2,500 flights in various machines of his own design. He made both biplanes and monoplanes – the latter were by far the most successful. Sadly, he died after a crash.

ANTHONY FOKKER (1890–1939)

The Dutchman's name became infamous as the "Fokker Scourge" in late 1915 because of his "Eindekker" monoplane, a fighter equipped with a forward-firing machine gun, making it lethal in the air.

WILBUR (1867–1912) AND ORVILLE (1871–1948) WRIGHT

They progressed through a series of gliders to the *Flyer 1*, for which they also built the engine and propellers. They made the first powered flights in 1903.

COUNT VON ZEPPELIN (1838–1917)

Von Zeppelin's first airship was the LZ 1 of 1900. By 1909, the first successful commercial air transport company was in operation. The loss of the *Hindenburg* in 1937 brought the age of airships to a sudden end.

LOUIS BLÉRIOT (1872–1936)

Frenchman Blériot shot to fame after crossing the English Channel in 1909, crash-landing in front of Dover Castle. His first experimental aircraft was an unsuccessful ornithopter (flapping wing) device.

THE VOISIN BROTHERS

Charles (1880–1912) and Gabriel (1882–1912) were the first to manufacture aircraft for others to buy and fly. Early in World War I, Voisin machines were used as primitive bombers.

HUGO JUNKERS (1859–1935)

The Junkers company pioneered metal construction with the J–1 Blechesel of 1915. Corrugated (for strength) metal skin became a Junkers trademark, and was used in the later trimotor Ju 52/3m.

SYDNEY CAMM (1893–1966)

The British designer's early designs include the Hawker Hart and Fury biplanes of the 1930s. The Hurricane monoplane fighter of World War II was the world's first eight-gun fighter. Later designs included the Hunter and P1127 jets.

IGOR SIKORSKY (1889–1972)

Russian by birth, in his early years Sikorsky designed aircraft such as *Le Grand*, the first four-engined airplane. Later in the US, he pioneered a flying boats and helicopters. The company is a helicopter maker today.

WILLY MESSERSCHMITT (1898–1978)

His company made over 35,000 109 fighters, plus many other types, including the Me 163 (first rocket-driven fighter) and Me 262 (first operational jet). Today the company is part of the German DASA group.

DONALD DOUGLAS (1892–1981)

Douglas formed his own company in 1920. Four years later two Douglas World Cruisers completed the first air flight around the world. Today the company lives on as the McDonnell Douglas Corporation.

ERNST HEINKEL (1888–1958)

Heinkel formed his company in 1922. His successes included the He 70 which set eight world records. The He 178 was the first jet, flying on August 27, 1939. During World War II, the company made bombers and fighters.

R. J. MITCHELL (1895–1937)

Mitchell designed a line of machines that included the Supermarine racing seaplanes of the 1930s. His Spitfire became famous and was considered the best-looking British fighter plane of World War II – 20,351 were made.

FRANK WHITTLE (1907–1996)

Whittle researched jet propulsion through the 1920s, and patented an engine concept in 1930. In 1937 he started up the first turbojet engine. His E28/29 experimental aircraft, powered by the W1 engine, took off in 1941.

ACES AND PLACES

THE TRUE HEROES OF AVIATION are those pilots who have shown extraordinary courage as pioneers of long-distance flight, as wartime aces, or as fearless test pilots. Their deeds, and the aircraft they flew, are remembered at air shows and museums all over the world.

SUPERSONIC ACE

One peacetime ace is pilot Chuck Yeager. In 1947 he boarded a B–29 bomber that carried a small rocket plane, the Bell X–1. At 12,000 ft (3,658 m), he climbed into the X–1, dropped clear of the B–29, fired the motor, and shot through the sound barrier and into the record books.

BARON MANFRED VON
RICHTHOFEN

TOP GUNS

Baron Manfred von Richthofen, known as the "Red Baron," shot down 80 enemy planes during World War I, and eventually met the same fate himself. In World War II, German pilot Major Erich Hartmann downed 352 enemy aircraft, an astonishing record that still stands today.

AMELIA EARHART

A modern replica of the Red Baron's famous aircraft, a bright red Fokker triplane.

ATLANTIC SPIRIT

In 1932, American pilot Amelia Earhart became the first woman to cross the Atlantic solo; she also set a record fastest time for the journey of 13½ hours. The danger of the crossing was heightened by a fire in the engine for most of the 2,000 mile (3,220 km) flight. Amelia's achievements were many in a flying career that ended mysteriously over the Pacific Ocean, five years later in 1937.

FAMOUS AIRCRAFT COLLECTIONS

Britain's Shuttleworth Collection boasts one of the world's best collections of veteran aircraft in flying condition. Other vintage collections include La Ferte Alais in France, and Old Rhinebeck in the US.

FIRST INTERNATIONAL AIR SHOW

The first international air show was staged at Reims, France in 1909. The fastest aircraft flew at about 47 mph (75 km/h).

BIGGEST AIRSHOW

In 1995, the American Oshkosh convention of the Experimental Aircraft Association (EAA) drew an estimated 830,000 people, and 12,000 visiting aircraft. An incredible 2,719 different machines performed displays throughout the week.

AMY JOHNSON

ACROSS THE WORLD

In 1930, British pilot Amy Johnson, then 22 years old, became the first woman to fly solo from England to Australia. The trip took 20 days, nearly breaking the standing record, despite two forced landings along the way.

AMAZING AIRCRAFT FACTS

IT IS ALMOST A CENTURY since the Wright brothers made their first flight. Since then, a galaxy of weird and wonderful aircraft has been invented. Some have been successful, many have not, though the future is sure to reveal more experimental aircraft.

AROUND THE WORLD
In 1986, Dick Rutan and Jeana Yeager accomplished one of the last great aviation feats, flying around the world, nonstop, without refueling. Fuel tanks were built into almost every part of the unusual-looking *Voyager* to give it the fuel capacity to make the trip.

RUTAN
VOYAGER

HUGE CAPACITY
The greatest load of passengers was 1,087 on a Boeing 747 in 1991. It was evacuating Ethiopian Jews from Addis Ababa to Israel.

PLANES WITHOUT PILOTS
The DarkStar is an unmanned air vehicle (UAV) designed to take off, fly up to 1,000 miles (1,600 km), and spy on enemy activity – all without a pilot. DarkStar looks like a spaceship from a sci-fi movie, with a saucerlike body and long, spindly wings.

AIR GIANTS
The biggest airships dwarfed anything in the skies, before or since. The famous *Graf Zeppelin* was more than three times as long as a Boeing 747 and flew all over the world, slowly but safely.

WORLD'S HEAVIEST GLIDER

In 1982, Captain Eric Moody was flying a British Airways Boeing 747 over Java, Indonesia, when volcanic ash caused all of the engines to fail. For 12 minutes Captain Moody glided the 330-ton 747 down from 37,000 ft (11,278 m), eventually restarting three engines and landing the plane safely.

WINDOWS IN THE WINGS

The 34-seat Junkers G38 of 1929 was a giant in its day, and had some amazing features, including observation windows in the leading edges of the wings and in the nose of the aircraft! Passengers could sit and enjoy a grandstand view of the world ahead.

OLDEST JET AIRLINER

A 1959-built Boeing 707, was still flying in 1996. In that period it had spent 89,920 hours (over 10 years!) in the air.

RECORD BREAKERS

BOEING 747–400

• The largest airliner is the Boeing 747–400.

• The smallest jet is the Silver Bullet with a wing span of 17 ft (5.2 m).

• The fastest airspeed in a winged aircraft was by William J. "Pete" Knight in 1967 who flew Mach 6.73: 4,520 mph (7,232 km/h) in the X–15A–2.

• The fastest jet airspeed is 2,193 mph (3,529 km/h) by Capt Eldon Joersz and Major George Morgan, Jr. in a Lockheed SR–71A Blackbird in the US in 1976.

• The fastest airliner is the Aerospatiale/BAe Concorde. It can cruise at up to Mach 2.2: 1,450 mph (2,333 km/h).

• The New York to London air record – 1 hr, 54 min, and 56.4 sec – was set in 1974 by a Lockheed SR–71A Blackbird.

• The longest duration in the air is 64 days, 22 hr, 19 min, and 5 sec by Robert Timm and John Cook in a Cessna 172 *Hacienda*. They covered a distance equivalent to six times around the world without landing.

• The country with the busiest airline system is the US.

• The busiest international air route is Paris to London.

• The new Hong Kong airport, due to open in 1998, will eventually have a capacity of 87.3 million passengers.

Resources

MUSEUMS

BELGIUM

**Koninklijk
Legermuseum/Musée
Royal de l'Armée**
Jubelpark 3/Parc du
Cinquantenaire 3
B-1040 Bruxelles
Traces the history of
Belgium's air arm and
has a good showing
of World War I
aircraft.

FRANCE

**Amicale Jean Baptiste
Salis**
Aerodrome de Cernay
91590 La Ferte Alais
A collection of
"flying condition"
historic aircraft.

**Musée de l'Air et de
l'Espace**
Aeroport du Bourget
BP173
93350 Le Bourget
Includes some great
aircraft from the pioneer
days and the Spad
biplane of French
fighter ace Georges
Guynemer.

GERMANY

Luftwaffen Museum
Marseille-Kaserne
W-2081 Appen
A history of the
German Air Force.

RUSSIA

**The National Air and
Space Museum**
Monino Airfield
Moscow
Features rarities such
as the 1960s-era
"Bounder" supersonic
bomber jet.

SWEDEN

**Flygvapenmuseum
Malmen**
Box 13 300
S 580 13 Linkoping
A history of the
Swedish Air Force
includes a near-
complete collection
of Saab aircraft.

SWITZERLAND

**Fleigermuseum
Dubendorf**
Postfach CH-8600
Dubendorf
Features a history of the
Swiss Air Force.

UNITED KINGDOM

The Aerospace Museum
RAF Cosford
Shifnal
Shropshire
TF11 8UP
Features many rare and
experimental aircraft,
both military and civil.

Fleet Air Museum
RNAS Yeovilton
Ilchester
Somerset
BA22 8HT
Here you can "fly"
on a simulator.

Imperial War Museum
Duxford Airfield
Duxford
Cambridgeshire
CB2 4QR
A large collection,
including the vast aircraft-
packed "superhangar."

**Royal Air Force
Museum**
Hendon
London
NW9 5LL
Probably the largest
military aviation museum
in the UK.

The Shuttleworth Collection
Old Warden Aerodrome
Biggleswade
Bedfordshire
SG18 9ER
A collection of early
aircraft including a Blériot
IX, Sopwith Pup, and
Bristol F2B.

UNITED STATES
**Confederate Air Force
American Airpower
Heritage Museum**
PO Box 62000
Midland, TX 79711
Most aircraft are World
War II vintage.

Intrepid Museum
1 Intrepid Square
West 46th Street and
12th Avenue
New York, NY 10036
A naval aviation
collection housed in the
USS *Intrepid*.

National Air and Space Museum
Independence Avenue
Washington, DC 20560
Includes pioneer aircraft
such as the Wright *Flyer*,
Bell X–1, X–15, and the
Rutan *Voyager*.

Pima Air and Space Museum
6000 East Valencia Road
Tucson, AZ 85706
The Arizona desert
preserves the aircraft in
rust-free condition,
though the sun bleaches
the paintwork.

Rhinebeck Aerodrome Museum
44 Stone Church Road
Rhinebeck, NY 12572
Aircraft from 1900 to
1935. Weekend air shows
from mid-June to Oct.

San Diego Aerospace Museum
2001 Pan American Plaza
Balboa Park,
San Diego, CA 92101
An excellent collection of
rare machines, including
the six-engine Hughes
H–1 "Spruce Goose"
flying boat.

US Air Force Museum
Wright Patterson Air
Force Base
1100 Spaatz Street
Dayton, OH 45433-7102
The world's largest
collection of military
aircraft, includes almost
every USAF type.

AIR DISPLAYS

**The Farnborough
International Air Show**
alternates with the Paris
Salon and is held in
September. It features the
latest British aircraft and
thousands of suppliers.

The Oshkosh, Wisconsin
show held in August is the
biggest display in the US.
Nearly a million visitors
fly or drive to the show.

The Paris Salon at Le
Bourget is held in June,
every two years, and is a
showcase for the French
aviation industry.

The Reno Air Races, in
Nevada during July, are
probably the world's
fastest displays.

**The Royal International
Air Tattoo**, in Fairford
during July, is the largest
public display in the UK.
The event features
hundreds of aircraft.

Internet users can obtain
world air show information
on http://www.deltaweb.
co.uk

Glossary

AERODYNAMIC
Aerodynamics is a branch of mechanics that deals with the forces exerted by gases in motion. An aircraft which, size-for-size, is faster than a rival is considered the more aerodynamic design.

AEROSPIKE ENGINE
New type of rocket engine that burns its fuel outside the engine, rather than in the bell-shaped extension cone of traditional motors.

AFTERBURNER
Power-boost equipment installed in many jet engines, especially combat types. Extra fuel is sprayed into the jet exhaust to increase thrust.

AILERON
Movable surface on the rear of each wing that controls rolling motion.

AIR SUPERIORITY
Control of the air, either by destruction of enemy aircraft, or by threatening to do so if they leave their bases.

AMPHIBIOUS AIRCRAFT
An aircraft that can take off from land or water, as required.

ANTENNA
Wire, rod or dish-shaped aerial used in sending or receiving radio, radar or TV transmissions.

ARTIFICIAL HORIZON
Cockpit instrument that shows whether an aircraft is in level flight or not. Essential when flying in clouds, when there is no visible horizon.

AUTOGYRO
Type of aircraft that uses helicopter-style rotors instead of conventional wings – but they are unpowered, so an autogyro cannot take off or land vertically.

BIPLANE
An aircraft with two sets of wings, mounted one above the other. The Wright *Flyer* and most aircraft of World War I were biplanes.

CANARD
Small set of foreplanes, set ahead of the main wing. Canards perform the same pitch control function as the rear-mounted elevators of most aircraft.

COBRA MANEUVER
Aerobatic movement performed by some Russian aircraft. To perform a cobra, a pilot raises the aircraft's nose beyond the vertical (the same angle as a cobra snake) for a moment, before tilting down again to resume normal flight.

COCKPIT
Command area of an aircraft, where the pilot sits. On bigger aircraft with two or more flight crew, it is called the flight deck, a term that also describes the flat top of an aircraft carrier.

CONTROL COLUMN
Cockpit hand control
that moves the ailerons
and elevators. The
rudder is controlled
by foot pedals.

CRUISE MISSILE
Air- or sea-launched
missile that can be
released some distance
from the target,
automatically finding
its way by using map
details stored in on-
board computers.

DELTA
Triangular aircraft
wing, named after the
Greek letter of the
same shape.

DIRIGIBLE
Literally, steerable; used
to describe engine-
driven airships, which
can be steered, rather
than balloons, which
drift with the wind.

DITCHING
To land on water in
an emergency.

DOGFIGHT
A fight at close quarters
between fighter aircraft.

EJECTOR SEAT
Gas- or rocket-powered
seat used for emergency
escapes. Normally an

ejector seat blasts
through the cockpit
canopy, after which seat
and pilot separate, the
pilot descending safely
using a parachute.

ELEVATOR
Rear-mounted,
horizontal tail surface
that controls pitching
motion. Delta-wing
aircraft are usually
equipped with elevons,
which combine the
functions of an aileron
and an elevator in one
control surface.

FLAP
Section of rear wing
that extends below and
behind during takeoff
and landing. It increases
lift and acts as a brake.

FLARE
Used in emergency
situations, a flare is a
device that burns
brightly as a distress
signal to alert rescuers.

FLIGHT DATA RECORDER
Fire and waterproof
recording device, also
known as the "black
box," it continuously
records technical
details during a flight,
such as the height,

speed, and course. If
recovered after a crash,
its information can be
used by researchers to
help determine the
cause of the accident.

FLIGHT PATH
The course through the
air of an aircraft, rocket
or projectile.

FLIGHT SIMULATOR
Mock-up of a cockpit,
with working controls
and an outside view
projected onto a screen.
Used especially to
practice emergency
procedures and to gain
experience of a new
aircraft type before
flying the real thing.

FLY-BY-WIRE
Control system that
uses electrical signals to
operate such controls as
elevator, ailerons, and
rudder. Previously these
were worked by rods
and cables.

FLYING BOAT
Aircraft with a boat-
shaped underbelly,
designed for water
operations.

FUSELAGE
The body of an
aeroplane.

G-FORCE
Apparent weight, compared to the force of gravity, 1G. A pilot pulling a high-speed turn may pull several Gs during the turn; free fall exerts no weight at all, hence zero-G.

GUNSHIP
Name for heavily armed battlefield helicopter. Also used for any heavily armed aircraft, such as the special C–47s used in the Vietnam War, nicknamed "Puff the Magic Dragon," for their firepower.

HANGAR
A large storage shed used for aircraft storage and maintenance.

HELIOGRAPH
Device for signalling (usually the dot-dash Morse code) by flashing the Sun's rays from a mirror.

MACH NUMBER
Named after the Austrian physicist Ernst Mach; describes speed compared to that of sound. Mach 1 is about 760 mph (1,224 km/h) at sea level, falling to about 660 mph (1,063 km/h) in the stratosphere. Mach 2 is twice the speed of sound and so on.

PALLET
Metal cargo case that fits into the underbelly hold of an airliner.

RADAR
Equipment that sends out a radio wave, receiving it back as a bounced "echo" from an object. Weather radar shows storm clouds; terrain-following radar shows the ground ahead of the aircraft.

RADOME
Protective housing for a radar antenna, made from a material that is transparent to radio waves. On aircraft, radomes are normally nose-mounted, though larger ones are occasionally mounted over the fuselage or under a wing.

RAM
Radar Absorbent Materials, used in making radar-proof aircraft. Typically made from carbon fibers mixed in a plastic coating, radar waves pass through the plastic and are scattered in all directions by the fibres.

RANGE
Distance an aircraft can fly without refueling. May be one-way to a destination, or half the distance for a return-to-base flight.

RECONNAISSANCE
Exploratory survey, as in making a spy flight to get information about enemy positions.

ROTOR
In helicopters, describes the spinning blades. Most helicopters have a large main rotor for lift and smaller tail rotor for controlling direction.

SENSOR BOOM
Metal tube with pickups for equipment measuring airspeed, altitude, temperature, and so on.

SONIC BOOM
Explosive sound made by an aircraft moving at or above the speed of sound.

SONOBUOY
Listening device that can pick up the sound of a passing submarine.

SQUADRON
A unit consisting of a number of aircraft and their crews. May be divided into "flights," and several squadrons may make up a "wing."

STEALTH
Technology used on an aircraft such as the B-2 bomber, which is designed to be nearly invisible to radar. Although it has a wingspan of over 172 ft (52 m), on a radar screen the B-2 appears no bigger than a seagull.

STREAMLINING
Special shaping of an aircraft that allows it to slip through the air with minimum drag.

SUPERCHARGER
Pump that forces more fuel/air mixture into a piston engine for a power boost.

SWING-WING
Aircraft that has movable wings – straight out for slow-speed takeoff and landing, swept-back for high-speed flight.

TORQUE
A force which causes rotation – in a helicopter, torque reaction from a single main rotor requires a tail rotor to counteract it.

TURBOJET
A type of jet engine with a turbine-driven air compressor that compresses air for fuel combustion. The resulting hot gases spin the turbine before forming the propulsive jet.

WINGLET
Upturned tip that smooths out the airflow past the wing. This reduces drag, so thus increasing speed slightly and lowering fuel consumption.

WING WARPING
Type of roll control used in some early aircraft. The rear of the wings were bent – warped – to perform the same function as the more usual ailerons, used since.

X-PLANE
Used to describe any highly experimental aircraft, and especially the American X-series machines that started with the X–1 of 1947.

ABBREVIATIONS:

CRT
Cathode Ray Tube

FBW
Fly-By-Wire

GPS
Global Positioning System

MAD
Magnetic Anomaly Detector

RADAR
Radio Direction and Ranging

RAM
Radar Absorbent Material

RLV
Reusable Launch Vehicle

SSTO
Single Stage to Orbit

UAV
Unmanned Air Vehicle

VP
Variable Pitch

WSO
Weapon Systems Operator

Index

Acknowledgments

Dorling Kindersley would like to thank:
Lynn Bresler for the index, Janet Allis,
Jacqui Burton, Sally Geeve, Nicki Studdart,
Steve Wong, Clare Watson, and Costantia
Kalantidi for design assistance, Caroline
Potts for picture library services.

Photographs by:
Peter Anderson, Martin Cameron, Peter
Chadwick, Andy Crawford, Mike
Dunning, David Exton, Lynton Gardiner,
Steve Gorton, Gary Kevin, Dave King,
Dave Rudkin, James Stevenson and
Martin Wilson.

Illustrations by:
Mike Gillah, Hans Jenssen, Stan Johnson,
and David Pugh.

Picture Credits
t=top c=center a=above b=below
l=left r=right.

The Publisher would like to thank the
following for their kind permission to
reproduce the photographs:
Aerospatiale 45tr; AI(R) 36bl, 39tr; Airbus
Industrie 25t, 31r, 39tl, 100cr, 101tl,
102–103c; Alpha Archive 43tl, 48br, 56tl,
64b, 98b, 112tl, bl, tr, 113cl, tr, 114cl, 115tl,
cr; BAe Defence Ltd 61b; Bell Boeing 85bl,
br; Boeing Commercial Airplane Group
27bl, 32–33, 40b, 41cr, b, 117tr; Boeing
Sikorsky 102bl; Bombadier Canadair 12br,
13bl, 37br, 55tr, cr, 57; Cessna Aircraft
Company 46–47; Dassault Aviation 13t,
67cl, 69t; Delta Collection 28bl, 29cr, 30b,
36r, 49tl, 54tl, 62bl, 64cl, 65t, 66b, 68tl,
76cl, b, 77br, 78tl, 79c, tr, 96–97, 112cl, cr,
br, 113tl, bl, cr, br, 114br; EH Industries
84br; Eurocopter/ Bristow Helicopters Ltd
83t, cr; Eurojet 20–21; Hughes Missile
Systems 69cr; Hulton Getty Picture
Collection Ltd 80br; Julian Humphries
10–11; Image Bank/ Eric Meola 13cr; Israel
Aircraft Industries Ltd 63tl, 67br; David
Jefferis 24tr, 42b, 43bl, tr, 44tl, cr, 52br,
53br, 57c; Kaman Aerospace Corp 83br;
Lockheed Martin 61t, c, 99t, 103cr, bl;
Magnum Photos/ Rene Burri 116crb; Mary
Evans Picture Library/ Firguier Nouveilles
de la Sciences 14bl, 15ca; McDonnell
Douglas Corp 40c, 58–59, 65bl, 69br, 83br,
86tr, 94tl, 101r; Ministry of Defence 12cl,
65r; NASA 98cr, 99cl; Northrop Grumman
Corp 67tr, 68–69c, 101cl, 103tl; Pilatus
31br; Raytheon 54bl, cr, 55bl, br;
Rediffusion Simulation 100bl; Dave Roberts
60b; Rockwell/Deutsche Aerospace 99r;
Saab/ J. Lindahl 37tr, Ake Andersson 63br;
Shorts 24br; Texas Instruments 88–89;
Westland Group 80–81, 84cl, 85t; Quadrant
Picture Library 91br.

Every effort has been made to trace the
copyright holders and we apologize in
advance for any unintentional omissions.
We would be pleased to insert the
appropriate acknowledgment in any
subsequent edition of this publication.